COVENANT
MARRIAGE

BUILDING COMMUNICATION & INTIMACY

COVENANT

MARRIAGE

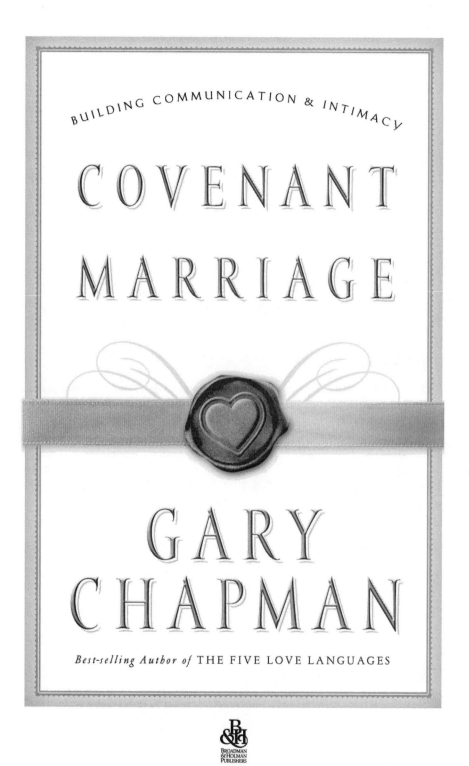

GARY
CHAPMAN

Best-selling Author of THE FIVE LOVE LANGUAGES

BROADMAN
& HOLMAN
PUBLISHERS

NASHVILLE, TENNESSEE

Published by Broadman & Holman Publishers,
Nashville, Tennessee

Dewey Decimal Classification: 306.81
Subject Heading: MARRIAGE

1 2 3 4 5 6 7 8 9 10 07 06 05 04 03

I dedicate this book to

Karolyn,
with whom I have been building a covenant marriage
for more than four decades.

CONTENTS

INTRODUCTION

In the contemporary world, few things are more important to the church than addressing the needs that exist in Christian marriages. In the past, many have felt that marriage enrichment was simply a sideline activity for the church, that once in awhile the church should do something to emphasize marriage. But with the increasing number of divorces among Christian couples and the alarming number of missionaries and pastors who are leaving the ministry because of marital failure, we realize that marriage enrichment is not a sideline. It is at the heart of the church's mission in today's world. If a couple cannot experience the saving power of Jesus Christ and the transformation of the inner man so they can gain a measure of freedom from self-centeredness and experience something of the love and joy that Christ came to give, and to share these in their marital relationship, they will not have the internal motivation to continue to be involved in evangelism and world missions.

For those who are married, marriage becomes the second most important relationship in life, the first and most important being one's relationship with God. Man's relationship with God is of utmost importance because it transcends time, and it greatly influences all other relationships. On the human level, the marriage relationship is seen as the most intimate of all relationships. It supercedes an individual's relationship with parents, for in marriage the Scriptures teach that we are to leave our parents. The marriage relationship is more abiding than the parent–child relationship, for eventually the children will leave. Also, the quality of the marriage relationship greatly influences the children positively or negatively.

The marriage relationship is so significant that God chose it as a picture of his relationship with his people. In the Old Testament, we are told that God saw himself as the husband of Israel (Isa. 54:5). In the New Testament, Christ is seen as the husband of the church (2 Cor. 11:2).

When a Christian has a healthy marriage, the whole world looks bright. When the marriage relationship is empty, it negatively affects all other aspects of life. The work of many churches has been greatly hampered by the deterioration of marriages. For example, it is difficult to motivate a husband to be active in evangelistic outreach when his marriage is in trouble. It is hard for him to be motivated to knock on someone's door and ask, "Wouldn't you like to become a Christian and be as miserable as I am?" Feeling hypocritical in such efforts, he chooses to avoid the church's visitation program.

For couples who have children, the marital relationship greatly affects their quality of parenting. A wife whose emotional needs are not met in the marriage may turn to the child for emotional affirmation. Investing her life in the child, she is totally devastated when that child leaves home. In the process, she may become a domineering mother who does not allow the child independence and freedom. Thus, the child is socially and emotionally handicapped upon entering adulthood. A loving and growing marriage is the greatest gift any couple can give their children. It is the most important of all parenting skills.

Communication and intimacy are two of the most important aspects of developing a growing marriage. The word *communication* is found in the dictionary between the words *commotion* and *community*. Many couples have experienced the commotion that has resulted from poor communication. Hopefully, they have also been blessed by the sense of community that develops when there is good communication. The idea of intimacy is at the very heart of the biblical concept of marriage. So intimate is the marriage relationship that the two are declared to become "one flesh" (Gen. 2:24). The word *one* in this verse is the same word used to describe God in Deuteronomy 6:4, which says, "Hear, O Israel: the LORD our God, the LORD is one!" (NKJV). The Hebrew word for *one* means "composite unity," as opposed to absolute unity. In the case of God, it is three who are one; in the case of marriage, two who are one. Apparently, God's desire is that the marriage relationship be extremely intimate. Such intimacy will sustain a marriage relationship even in our modern world.

How do we attain such intimacy in marriage? For the Christian, the answer grows out of the following assumptions:

- The lasting answers to marital growth are found in the Bible.
- Your relationship with God greatly enhances your marriage relationship.
- Communication is the primary vehicle by which two persons become one in the marriage relationship.
- Marital oneness does not mean that we lose our individuality.
- Sex was God's idea; thus, his guidelines are best.
- Sex is an important part of a growing marriage relationship.
- The idea of biblical oneness involves not only sex but also intellectual, spiritual, emotional, and social oneness.

These are the assumptions upon which the material in this volume is based.

Perhaps no relationship demands so much Christian discipline as marriage. Often, premarital preparation involves only an informal conversation with a pastor while the starry-eyed couple makes preparations for the wedding. The couple makes a lifetime commitment to share virtually every aspect of their lives with each other, but they are ill prepared to do this. *Covenant Marriage* is concerned particularly with helping Christians understand what the Bible teaches and how it can be applied to everyday married life. In this volume, we seek to address the following needs:

The need for clear, biblically-based principles for building a Christian marriage. Seeing that the divorce rate is the highest it has been in the history of our country, it is clear that secular principles have not worked. We are forced to look for a different approach. *Covenant Marriage* declares that that approach should be biblical. Even among Christians, we have sometimes misinterpreted the Bible by reading our cultural patterns into the biblical text rather than letting the Bible be the standard whereby we measure our cultural norms.

The need for individuality within the marriage relationship. The Scriptures make it very clear that though "two become one flesh," we do not lose our individuality. Ultimately, we must face God as individuals. We will each give an account for our own lives, the way we have invested our time, energy, and money and whether we have had a personal relationship with Jesus Christ and have sought to follow him. In marriage, we are a team. That team is composed of two individuals, and we must never fail to recognize our individuality.

The need to understand that life is more than having a good marriage. The Christian's ultimate call is not the call to develop a good marriage; the Christian's call is to be a disciple of Jesus Christ. For many of us, at least a good portion of our adult lives will be spent in a marriage relationship. If we follow biblical guidelines for marriage, this relationship can enhance our growth as disciples of Christ. It can provide for us an opportunity to practice such principles as servanthood and unconditional love. But as Christians, we must remember that marriage is not an end in itself. Individually and as a couple, we are to give ourselves to ministering in our community and around the world.

The need to discover biblical principles for handling conflict, anger, and misunderstandings, and to learn skills in applying these principles. What does the Bible say about anger? How are we to handle the normal conflicts in a marriage relationship? How do we deal with misunderstandings that commonly occur? *Covenant Marriage* will address these questions.

The need to understand the positive, biblical view of human sexuality. In our contemporary sex-saturated society, it is tragic that so few Christians have a clear picture of the biblical perspective on sexuality. Some in our society have taken a gift of God—sexuality—and made it a god. They worship at the altar of sex. Time, energy, and effort are expended in trying to find sexual fulfillment. Such idolatry never brings satisfaction. It is the Christian who knows God—the author of sex—and who discovers the proper role of sexual fulfillment within a marriage who will find true sexual satisfaction.

The need for a definition of love that is biblical rather than secular. The secular concept of love focuses on feelings. It has been said that "love is the feeling that you feel when you feel a feeling like you've never felt before." In the Bible, love is not basically a feeling but an attitude expressed in appropriate behavior. It is the attitude that chooses to build up another, to put their interest above your own interest. Love is something you choose to do. This does not mean the Bible makes no place for feelings. The Bible speaks of romantic love, and, in fact, understanding the broader biblical perspective on love will enhance romantic love.

The need to develop patterns of communication that can build intimacy and lead to ministry. Marriage is designed by God to be the most intimate of human relationships, but such intimacy cannot be obtained without wholesome responsible communication. We must identify the negative patterns of communication that keep us from intimacy, and we must build positive patterns that will draw us together. As a team committed to each other and growing in our understanding and concern for each other, we can then reach out to minister to a needy world. Our love and intimacy may provide the strongest attraction to the non-Christian world—a world that desperately seeks love. Jesus said, "All people will know that you are My disciples, if you have love for one another" (John 13:35). This evidence of our Christianity is not only to be visible in the church but in a Christian marriage.

These are the needs I seek to address in the following pages. It is my sincere desire that what you read will strengthen your own marriage in the areas of communication and intimacy as well as help you feel better equipped to minister to other couples in your church or community who may be struggling in their marriages. Let's begin by looking at the difference between a *contract* marriage and a *covenant* marriage.

CHAPTER ONE

CONTRACT MARRIAGES

In spite of the fact that the concept of covenant is seen throughout the Bible, we do not often use the word *covenant* in our conversation. Most of us have little understanding of the word. When we think of marriage, we usually do so in terms of a contract rather than a covenant. In reality, the two words are quite different. In this chapter, I want to first focus on contract marriages.

Understanding Contracts

Ours is a contract-oriented society. We understand contracts and often hear people say, "Get it in writing," meaning "Get a legal contract signed." With a contract you can be more certain that the person or company will live up to their claims.

Many Christian couples have brought this contract mentality into their marriages. They busy themselves with making contracts and trying to force each other into living up to them. Unfortunately, this kind of marriage stimulates resentment, hurt, and anger and eventually leads some couples to divorce. Let's explore this contract mentality.

Basically, a contract is an agreement between two or more persons specifying that one will do something if the other will do something. For example, the bank agrees to allow me to drive a car if I will make the monthly payments. If I break my part of the contract, the bank has the legal right to repossess my car. Our society is built upon the concept of contracts. We make rental contracts, sales contracts, and service contracts regularly.

Some of our contracts are legally binding; others are morally binding. If my wife and I agree that I will wash the dishes if she will cook the meal, we have made an informal contract. No court of law will ever hold us to that contract, but as persons of integrity, we each feel a sense of moral responsibility to keep our end of the bargain. Any informal contract is only as good as the character of the persons who make it. Many relationships have been fractured or broken because someone failed to keep an agreement. If it is a legal contract, then one of the parties may sue the other in an effort to gain a fair settlement. In an informal, non-legal contract, the broken contract becomes a source of argument, accusation, and sometimes verbal or physical abuse by which we try to motivate the other person to keep the agreement he/she made.

Legally, marriage is a contract with certain rights and responsibilities. But we must distinguish between legal marriage and covenant marriage. In a legal marriage, if one party does not live up to the contract, then legal actions force them to do so or to end the marriage with an equitable settlement. A society could not exist without laws regulating marriage relationships, so in this sense, marriage is a contract. For a Christian, however, marriage is more than this; it is a covenant.

Contracts are important. Most married couples have made numerous ones with each other through the years: "If you will get the children to bed, I will clean up the kitchen." "If you will wash the windows on the outside, I will wash them on the inside." "If you will vacuum and dust, I will mow the grass and trim the shrubs." There is nothing wrong with making such contracts. In fact, such agreements are a part of any couple's life. These agreements help us get things done, using our different abilities and interests to our mutual benefit.

The problem arises when we come to view our marriage *only* as a contract or a series of contracts. When this happens, we have become totally secular in our thinking and have abandoned the biblical view of marriage. The Bible views marriage ultimately as a covenant although contracts may be an important part of carrying out our covenant.

Contract Characteristics

There are five general characteristics of contracts.

1. Contracts Are Most Often Made for a Limited Period of Time

When we decide to lease a car, we sign a contract for a set number of years. If we rent an apartment, typically the rental contract is for a minimum of six months or one year. When we purchase a house, we sign a loan contract for fifteen to thirty years. Almost all legal contracts are made for a specified period of time. If it is broken by either party, there is a penalty to be paid. Contracts are usually made with the idea that the arrangement will be mutually beneficial for the parties involved. If, however, the circumstances change, we may decide to break the contract and suffer the penalties.

Although most marriage ceremonies involve the commitment "so long as we both shall live" or "till death do us part," many couples give a contractual interpretation to these covenantal words. What they are really saying is, "We are committed to each other so long as this relationship is mutually beneficial for us. If in two years or twenty this marriage ceases to be mutually beneficial, then we can break the contract and suffer the penalties." This contract mentality predisposes the couple to divorce when the relationship comes upon hard times.

2. Contracts Most Often Deal with Specific Actions

When you buy a new appliance, you will likely be offered an extended service contract. This stipulates that if you will pay the fee, the company will service your appliance for a certain period of time in specified ways. Most service contracts will cover "parts and labor," with certain exceptions. Read the fine print and you will know precisely what the company has agreed to do.

Most informal contracts made within the marriage also deal with specific actions. "If you will keep the children tonight while I go shopping, I will keep them tomorrow while you play softball." In this arrangement the couple is not establishing general roles in the marriage relationship; they are simply contracting for specific events or activities. Such informal agreements can be a positive way of negotiating the details of family life. If made with a spirit of love and concern for each other, they can in fact be a way of implementing a covenant marriage relationship.

3. Contracts Are Based on an "If . . . , Then . . . ." Mentality

If you are willing to sign a one-year contract and pay the monthly service charge, *then* we will give you a free cell phone with no "roaming charges." This is the language of a contract. It is a negotiating tool based on a willingness to give in order to get. Though I would not have admitted it at the time, I must confess that it is the mentality with which I entered marriage more than forty years ago. I was willing to make Karolyn happy if she would make me happy. She didn't and I didn't; therefore, our struggle was deep, fierce, and painful in the first several years of our marriage. In talking to other couples, I have discovered that my wife and I were not alone in our contractual mentality. However deeply spiritual we claimed to be, we were far more secular in our approach to marriage.

4. Contracts Are Motivated by the Desire to Get Something We Want

Almost always the person who initiates the discussion about a contract wants something. This desire is the motivation for trying to make a contract with the other person. The salesman is the contract seeker. He/she initiates a conversation with the desire to "make a sale" and reap the benefits. They may "believe in the value of their product." They may also believe that the product will "serve you well." But if they did not desire the benefits of the sales contract, they would not long be a salesman. In marriage, the same principle is true. If I initiate a conversation with my wife, expressing a willingness to do something for her if she will do something for me, you can be certain my conversation was motivated by something I wanted. When I say to her, "If I mow the grass this afternoon, would you have time to iron my blue shirt for the party tonight?" I am trying to "strike a deal" that will get me a blue shirt for the party.

5. Contracts Are Sometimes Unspoken and Implicit

One husband said, "We have never discussed it, but both of us know our agreement. If I will do her favorite project, she will make life more exciting for me. It is also understood that if I do not do what she wants, then she can make life miserable for me." This husband is illustrating a contract marriage even though the contract has never been verbalized. He and his wife have established an arrangement without conversation.

る る る

While marriage is a legal contract to be honored, and informal contracts within marriage often help us effectively use our differing skills to our mutual benefit, Christian marriage is much more than a contract. This "much more" is to be discovered in the word *covenant*.

CHAPTER TWO

COVENANT MARRIAGES

Why the term *covenant marriage?* Because it most clearly denotes the uniqueness of Christian marriage. *Covenant* is a biblical term. God is a covenant-making God.

Covenants in Scripture

The first time the word *covenant* is used in the Bible is in Genesis 6:18. God told Noah that because of man's wickedness, God would destroy all life on earth. Then God said to Noah, "But I will establish my covenant with you, and you will enter the ark—you and your sons and your wife and your sons' wives with you." God went on to indicate that he would also preserve the animal world through the ark that Noah built.

God took the initiative in making the covenant. The covenant was for Noah's benefit. He accepted God's covenant and built the ark. Noah entered into covenant with God to do what he could do (build the ark) and accept the gift of God's grace—something he could not do for himself (save himself from the flood waters). God's motive was not to get an ark for himself;

he did not need one, but Noah did. Noah's willingness to build the ark indicated his acceptance of God's covenant offer of deliverance.

The Old Testament tells us that God went on to make covenants with Abraham (Gen. 17:3–8) and Moses (Exod. 19:3–6). God confirmed his covenant with David (2 Sam. 7:12–29), and the prophets often reminded Israel of their covenant relationship with God (Jer. 31; Ezek. 37; Hos. 2).

The New Testament reveals Jesus as the Messiah who fulfilled the old covenant and instituted the new covenant (Matt. 26:28; Luke 22:20). The New Testament writers in turn developed and used the covenant concept (2 Cor. 3:6; Gal. 3:15; Heb. 7:22; 8:6; 13:20).

In the Bible we not only find God's covenant with his people but also observe people making covenants with other people. For example, in 1 Samuel 18:1–3, Jonathan makes a covenant with David. In Ruth 1:16–17, Ruth makes a covenant with Naomi.

Therefore, we should not be surprised to discover that in the Bible, marriage is also viewed as a covenant between a man and woman. When the writer of Proverbs warns his son against becoming involved with a wayward wife who "abandons the companion of her youth and forgets the covenant of her God," he indicates clearly that marriage is a sacred covenant (Prov. 2:16–17). God often depicted his relationship with Israel as a covenantal marriage relationship. Through the prophet Ezekiel, he described Israel as an adulterous wife for whom he yearns. "I gave you my solemn oath and entered into a covenant with you, declares the Sovereign LORD, and you became mine" (Ezek. 16:8). Through the prophet Malachi, God expressed his displeasure with divorce and indicates that "the LORD is acting as the witness between you and the wife of your youth, because you have broken faith with her, though she is your partner, the wife of your marriage covenant" (Mal. 2:14, 16). Jesus himself clearly viewed marriage as a lifelong covenantal relationship (Matt. 19:4–9).

Covenant Characteristics

What then is the meaning of this word *covenant,* which is woven so integrally into the fabric of Scripture? A covenant, like a contract, is an agreement made between two or more persons, but the nature of the agreement is quite different. Let me begin by sharing five characteristics of a covenant relationship.

1. Covenants Are Initiated for the Benefit of the Other Person

Read the covenant Jonathan made with David: "From that day Saul kept David with him and did not let him return to his father's house. And Jonathan made a covenant with David because he loved him as himself. Jonathan took off the robe he was wearing and gave it to David, along with his tunic, and even his sword, his bow and his belt" (1 Sam. 18:2–4). Notice that Jonathan took the initiative in this covenant. His first act was an act of giving: his robe, tunic, sword, bow, and belt. Jonathan's motivation for making a covenant with David grew from his love for David and not from a selfish desire to manipulate David to do something for him.

Read the words of Ruth as she made her covenant with Naomi: "Don't urge me to leave you or to turn back from you. Where you go I will go, and where you stay I will stay. Your people will be my people and your God my God. Where you die I will die, and there I will be buried" (Ruth 1:16–17). In verses 11–13, Naomi had already made it clear to Ruth that she had nothing to offer her. Yet Ruth's commitment to Naomi clearly grew from her concern for Naomi's well-being. While David and Naomi's sense of commitment to the covenant was fully as strong as that of Jonathan and Ruth, they did not initiate the covenant. Covenants are born from a desire to minister to the other person, not to manipulate the person or to get something.

This aspect of a covenant relationship is further illustrated by God's covenant with Noah, to which we alluded earlier. God took the initiative to spare Noah and his family from his judgment. "Noah was a righteous man, blameless among the people of his time, and he walked with God" (Gen. 6:9). But God's covenant with Noah was not made in order to motivate Noah to love him, but rather from God's concern for Noah's well-being.

After the flood, God made another covenant with Noah and his descendants: "I establish my covenant with you: Never again will all life be cut off by the waters of a flood; never again will there be a flood to destroy the earth. . . . This is the sign of the covenant I am making. . . . I have set my rainbow in the clouds, and it will be the sign of the covenant between me and the earth" (Gen. 9:11–13). In this covenant, nothing was expected of Noah. God simply declared his intention for the future and gave a sign of the covenant. When we see the sign of the rainbow, we are reminded of that ancient covenant.

Therefore, in a covenant marriage each spouse is committed to the other's well-being. Obviously, if both of them keep the covenant, then both of them will benefit, but the motivation and the attitude is not self-gratification but giving of self for the other's well-being.

Some will say, "Let's be honest. How many of us entered marriage motivated by this deep desire to benefit the person we were about to marry?" Well, then, let's *be* honest. I wish I could say that my supreme motivation when I got married was to make my wife happy. In all honesty, I must admit that most of my thoughts centered on how happy I was going to be once we got married. Thus, I am admitting that for many years my marriage was not a covenant marriage. My behavior in the early years made it clear that I was operating on a contract mentality. I had clear ideas about what she should do; and if she would do those things, I would be happy. I busied myself with trying to entice her to follow my agenda. The first several years of our marriage were extremely painful and frustrating. I don't want to judge others, but my guess is that our marriage was not radically different from many marriages today.

What is more important than the attitude with which we entered marriage is the attitude we have today. I am happy to report that at this juncture in my marriage, I am deeply concerned about my wife's well-being. I spend a great deal of time and energy seeking to understand her needs and find ways to minister to her. And fortunately, she has the same attitude toward me. We would be quick to acknowledge that we are not perfect, but we would also acknowledge that this attitude of looking out for the interests of the other has radically changed the nature of our relationship. Perhaps that is why we are so strongly committed to the concept of covenant marriage.

2. In Covenant Relationships, People Make Unconditional Promises

God's covenant with Noah and his descendants was not predicated on their behavior. This does not mean that God's covenant does not involve a response. In God's original covenant with Noah in Genesis 6, Noah was asked to build an ark in which he, his family, and the animals would be saved. Theoretically, if Noah had not built the ark, he would not have been saved. Thus, a covenant assumes a mutual response by the other party, but the covenant is not conditioned on the other person's behavior. Noah's response indicated his acceptance of God's covenant.

The strong words of Ruth's commitment to Naomi are not conditional statements. She did not say, "I will go with you to your homeland and see how things turn out. If I find out that things go well, I will stay, but if not, I will return to my people." No such conditions were a part of Ruth's covenant with Naomi. On the contrary, her covenant with Naomi was unconditional.

At first sight, some of God's covenants seem to be couched in conditional terms. For example, Exodus 19:5–6: "Now if you obey me fully and keep my covenant, then out of all nations you will be my treasured possession. Although the whole earth is mine, you will be for me a kingdom of priests and a holy nation."

It may appear that God's covenant was conditioned upon their obedience. In reality, that was not the case. God was committed to make Israel a kingdom of priests and a holy nation. God did not withdraw his covenant when they refused to obey his commands. The fact is, however, that Israel could not enjoy the benefits of God's covenant if they did not cooperate with him. They could not be a holy nation and a nation of priests unless they walked in holiness with God and were available to minister to other nations. The Old Testament records that often they did not experience this kind of loyalty to God. But God continued to reach out generation after generation to work with those within the nation of Israel who would be responsive to him and who would live out his covenant. The believing remnant both in Old Testament and New Testament times were the ones who experienced the benefit of God's covenant with Israel. Therefore, God's covenant promises were unconditional. However, the fruit of the covenant could not be enjoyed unless Israel was willing to respond to God's covenant.

Let me illustrate the principle in a marriage relationship. A husband comes to recognize that he has been giving little quality time to his wife—to listen to her concerns, joys, and struggles. He makes a covenant to become a faithful listener so that he may be aware of his wife's ideas and feelings and thus seek to minister to her. If his commitment is unconditional, his listening will not be predicated upon her moods, the manner in which she speaks, or what she shares. He will be committed to listening, no matter what. For his wife to receive the benefit of this covenant, however, she must be willing to talk and be willing to share her thoughts and ideas. If she refuses to talk, his commitment to listening will be frustrated but not revoked. That is, he has not withdrawn his covenant; she is failing to experience the benefit of his covenant by her refusing to talk.

Most of God's covenants with us require a response on our part in order to enjoy the benefit of God's covenant. But God's covenant is never based on our response. For example, God is committed to forgiving us our sins, and that covenant is unconditional. In order for us to experience God's forgiveness, however, we must be willing to acknowledge our sin. As the apostle John says, "If we confess our sins, He is faithful and righteous to forgive us our sins and to cleanse us from all unrighteousness" (1 John 1:9). God's covenant promise to forgive us is not conditioned by our response. God has made full provision for our sins, and he stands fully ready to forgive at any moment. God will not withdraw his covenant promise, but if individually we are to experience the benefit of this promise, we must be willing to respond in confession and faith in Christ.

Thus, covenant marriages are characterized by unconditional promises. In traditional wedding vows, the covenant we make with each other is couched in unconditional terms. For example, many ceremonies include this question: "Wilt thou have this woman to be thy wedded wife? To live together in the holy estate of matrimony; wilt thou love her, comfort her, honor, and keep her, in sickness and in health, and forsaking all others, keep thou only unto her so long as you both shall live?" To which the husband responds, "I will." And the wife makes a similar pledge to the husband.

This is the language of covenant marriage, not contract marriage. Sadly, too many times after couples have verbalized a covenant relationship, they practice a contract marriage in which giving is conditioned on the spouse's positive behavior.

3. Covenant Relationships Are Based on Steadfast Love

The phrase "steadfast love" is the best translation of the Old Testament word *hesed* and the New Testament word *agape*. The characteristic of a steadfast love is at the center of covenant marriage. Sometimes the word *hesed* is translated "covenant." Most often, however, it is translated "loving-kindness." For example, "The LORD's lovingkindnesses indeed never cease, for His compassions never fail. They are new every morning; great is Thy faithfulness" (Lam. 3:22–23 NASB). As Christians, we find great security in knowing that God is a loving God and that his love is not fickle. We do not have to wonder what God's attitude toward us will be tomorrow. We know that it will be the same as it is today. His love never ceases.

In the New Testament, such love is described the following way: "Love is patient; love is kind. Love does not envy; is not boastful; is not conceited; does not act improperly; is not selfish; is not provoked; does not keep a record of wrongs; finds no joy in unrighteousness, but rejoices in the truth; bears all things, believes all things, hopes all things, endures all things. Love never ends" (1 Cor. 13:4–8).

We make contracts with almost anyone, even an unknown salesperson, but covenants are made only with those with whom we have loving relationships. Consider Jonathan's covenant with David: "Jonathan became one in spirit with David, and he loved him as himself. . . . And

Jonathan made a covenant with David because he loved him as himself" (1 Sam. 18:1, 3). Jonathan did not make a covenant with David in order to establish a relationship; the covenant grew from a loving relationship that was already established.

God's covenant with Noah reflected his love for Noah as well as Noah's response to that love: "Noah was a righteous man, blameless among the people of his time, and he walked with God" (Gen. 6:9). God did not arbitrarily decide to make a covenant with Noah. The covenant was based on a love relationship that already existed. When we stand before the minister at the marriage altar, we are not there to make a covenant in order to trap the other person into a relationship. We are there because we have already established a loving relationship. The covenant we make before God and witnesses is a covenant that grows from our love for each other.

God's steadfast love motivates us to enter into covenant with him. We know in our hearts that God is committed to our best interest. Therefore, with confidence we can commit our lives to loving and serving him. In covenant marriage, it is much the same. We enter our marriage with a sense that we are loved and that we love each other; thus, we can freely commit ourselves to each other for life. We are then responsible for maintaining this attitude of love throughout the marriage.

Obviously, this is not love as a romantic feeling. This love is something far deeper. Steadfast love does have an emotional element, but it is primarily a way of thinking and behaving toward one's spouse. Steadfast love is choosing to have positive regard for your spouse, choosing to focus on his/her positive characteristics, and expressing appreciation to him or her for these characteristics. It is doing things for him or her that will express this positive attitude.

Steadfast love refuses to focus on the negative aspects of one's spouse. All of us discover certain things about our spouse that we perceive as negative. We don't deny them. On the contrary, we discuss them, especially if there is the potential for change. Yet steadfast love refuses to dwell on these negative aspects. The violation of this principle has destroyed many marriages. Few people can survive the constant harassment and condemnation of a spouse. Such condemnation does not encourage one to change, but rather to give up. When we focus on the positive aspects of the spouse and give verbal affirmation, he or she is far more likely to continue to grow.

How does all of this affect our emotions? When the husband or wife chooses to express steadfast love toward his or her spouse, positive feelings are generated. The more you express affirmation and appreciation for the positive traits in your spouse, the stronger will become their positive feelings toward you. On the other hand, the more you focus on his or her failures and frailties, the more negative will become their feelings toward you. Our feelings are affected by our thoughts and our words. Tell yourself what a horrible spouse you have; rehearse for yourself all of her negative traits, and you will end in depression. On the other hand, focus on her positive traits; tell yourself—and her—how wonderful she is. Then enjoy to the fullest your spouse, and you will find positive feelings emerging from within.

Steadfast love is a choice. That's why Paul commanded husbands to love their wives (Eph. 5:25) and challenged wives to learn to love their husbands (Titus 2:4). Something that can be commanded, taught, and learned is not beyond our control. We choose our attitudes toward our spouse. The attitude of steadfast love is the single most important factor in a covenant marriage. In fact, choosing to have positive regard for one's spouse, to think of him/her in positive terms, will greatly affect the nature of the couple's communication.

If we grew up without feeling much positive regard from our parents, such love becomes extremely important in a marriage relationship. Few things are more edifying to a married person than the steadfast love of his spouse. That deep inner sense that we are loved by our spouse and that their attitude toward us is positive goes a long way in building self-esteem and helping us accomplish our potential for God and for doing good in the world.

4. Covenant Relationships View Commitments as Permanent

Read again the words of Ruth in her covenant with Naomi: "Don't urge me to leave you or to turn back from you. Where you go I will go, and where you stay I will stay. Your people will be my people and your God my God. Where you die I will die, and there I will be buried. May the LORD deal with me, be it ever so severely, if anything but death separates you and me" (Ruth 1:16–17). We cannot read these words without hearing the ring of permanence. So beautiful are these words that they often appear in marriage ceremonies.

Consider the words in God's covenant with Noah: "This is the sign of the covenant I am making between me and you and every living creature with you, a covenant for all generations to come. . . . Never again will the waters become a flood to destroy all life. Whenever the rainbow appears in the clouds, I will see it and remember the everlasting covenant between God and all living creatures of every kind on the earth" (Gen. 9:12, 15–16). Every time we see a rainbow in the sky, we are reminded that God's covenants are permanent.

Then there is God's covenant with Abraham: "The whole land of Canaan, where you are now an alien, I will give as an everlasting possession to you and your descendants after you; and I will be their God" (Gen. 17:8). Whatever one's view of the Middle East, most will admit that it is phenomenal that the nation of Israel was reestablished in 1948 as a homeland for Abraham's descendants. God's covenants are permanent.

The permanence of human covenants is also illustrated in Jonathan's covenant relationship with David. The covenant was made when David was young and long before he became king of Israel. Years later, after Jonathan's death, we find David asking, "Is there anyone still left of the house of Saul to whom I can show kindness for Jonathan's sake?" (2 Sam. 9:1). It was discovered that Jonathan had a crippled son named Mephibosheth still living, so David brought him to his own house and cared for him the rest of his life. David's covenant with Jonathan was permanent, transcending Jonathan's death. David wanted to show his kindness to Jonathan's son because he had a covenant relationship with Jonathan.

The country-western song asks, "Whatever happened to *forever?*" There was a time when a young man could go off to war, return four years later, and know that his father and mother would still be married. Now he goes off to college for one semester and returns to find that his parents have dissolved their marriage of thirty years. It seems that the prevalent thoughts of contemporary culture are that we lease our apartments on an annual contract, and we lease our cars for three years—why should marriage be any different?

"Till death do us part" or "So long as we both shall live," common statements in marriage ceremonies, are statements of covenant. Unquestionably, the covenant is meant to be permanent. This is not a contract for the next five years or until we find a "justifiable reason" to end the marriage. Christian marriage is a commitment to permanence.

Some may raise the question, "Should a Christian stay in a marriage that is destructive simply because the Bible holds up the ideal of a permanent monogamous relationship?" Such a question is easy to answer from an ivory tower, but it is more difficult to answer in the throes of daily pain. Unquestionably, the biblical ideal is one man and one woman married to each other for life. As Christians, we must not lower this ideal. Does this mean, however, that a wife is to remain in a marriage where she is physically abused every weekend by a drunken husband? Shall she remain in that marriage "till death do us part"? The answer to this question lies in the fifth characteristic of a covenant.

5. Covenant Relationships Require Confrontation and Forgiveness

Trace God's covenants with his people throughout the Old Testament, first with Noah (Gen. 9), then Abraham (Gen. 17), Moses (Exod. 19), Joshua (Josh. 24), David (2 Sam. 7), and others, and you will find that God's people often failed to live up to their covenant commitments to God. With even a casual reading of the Old Testament, we marvel that Israel could fail so often. Did God abandon his people because of their failures? Very clearly, the answer is no. On the other hand, did God ignore their failures? Again, the answer is no. God always confronted Israel with failures, but he stood ready to forgive.

These two responses—confrontation and forgiveness—are essential in a covenant marriage. Confrontation means holding the other person responsible for his/her actions. Forgiving means a willingness to lift the penalty and continue a loving, growing relationship.

This principle is summarized in Psalm 89, which speaks of God's covenant with David to establish God's kingdom forever. He says, "If his sons forsake My instruction and do not live by My ordinances, if they dishonor My statutes and do not keep My commandments, then I will call their rebellion to account with the rod, their sin with blows. But I will not withdraw My faithful love from him or betray My faithfulness. I will not violate My covenant or change what My lips have said. Once and for all I have sworn an oath by My holiness; I will not lie to David. His offspring will continue forever, and his throne like the sun before Me, like the moon established forever, a faithful witness in the sky" (vv. 30–37).

God's response to man's failure has always been confrontation and a willingness to forgive. Our failure does not cause God to withdraw his covenant. Rather, God makes provision for our failure. This does not mean that failure is treated lightly by God. The cross of Christ is forever God's statement of the costliness of forgiveness. Still, a covenant relationship with God would be impossible if God did not make provision for man's failure. In human relationships it is no different. None of us is perfect. We will sometimes fail one another. We will fail to live up to the covenants we have made with each other. Such failure need not destroy the covenant, but it does call for confrontation and forgiveness.

Ignoring the failures of your spouse is not the road to marital growth. "Grin and bear it" is not the language of covenant marriage. A person committed to a covenant marriage says, "I love you too much to remain silent when I see you breaking our covenant. What you are doing hurts me deeply, but I am willing to forgive you. Can't we please renew our covenant?"

Such covenant renewals are seen throughout God's relationship with his people. Examples are Joshua 1:16–18 and Joshua 24:14–28. For today's Christian, the same forgiveness is offered in 1 John 1:9: "If we confess our sins, He is faithful and righteous to forgive us our sins and to cleanse us from all unrighteousness." Note that although God's forgiveness is offered, it is not experienced until we are willing to confess our sins.

Likewise in a covenant marriage, each of us is to have a willingness to forgive, but forgiveness cannot be experienced and the relationship restored unless we are willing to be responsible for our actions and acknowledge our failures. Covenant marriage is marked by a commitment to responsible living and a willingness to forgive when our spouse fails.

Some individuals find confronting to be difficult. Past experiences have encouraged them to withdraw when they are wronged rather than to confront. We must understand that *confrontation* is not a bad word, nor does it need to be done in a harsh or ugly way. Confronting is simply love's way of trying to have an intimate marriage. It is in sharing your sense of being wronged and the pain of being hurt that gives your spouse an opportunity either to clarify his actions and thus help you understand that his action was not wrong or to acknowledge the wrongness of his behavior and ask your forgiveness.

There will be failures in every marriage. Although our covenants with each other have been seriously made, we will sometimes fail to live up to those covenant commitments. A good marriage is not destroyed by some failures, but a good marriage will be destroyed if we are not willing to deal with our failures and renew our covenant. Like Jacob in the Old Testament, we need to go back to Bethel and renew our covenant with God (Gen. 35:1–15). In marriage, we must also renew our covenant from time to time.

The spirit of forgiveness is fully as important as the willingness to confront. Some individuals will find it difficult to forgive. They are the kind of people who are hard on themselves and therefore may be hard on others. They hold high standards for themselves; they tend to be perfectionists. Because they require a lot of themselves, they also require much of others. These people need to understand that forgiveness is a part of all covenant marriage relationships. They need also to understand that forgiveness is not a feeling but rather a promise. Forgiveness is the promise that I will no longer hold that failure against you. You have confessed it, and I will lift the penalty and treat you as though you had not failed. This is the forgiveness God gives us when we accept Christ's sacrifice for our sins. It is the forgiveness that we are able to give others because we have been forgiven.

&a &a &a

Just as God's covenant with his people was renewed and expanded with different individuals in different generations throughout the Old and New Testaments, our covenants with each other in marriage need to be renewed and expanded as we move through the years. What covenant commitments did you make when you married each other? Perhaps it would be valuable to review your wedding ceremony again. What covenant commitments have you made to each other since your wedding? Perhaps you need to make new covenant commitments to each other. Perhaps you need to review the covenants you have already made to each other. You may discover that you have treated your marriage more as a contract than a covenant. Contracts may be a healthy part of a covenant marriage, but contracts alone do not provide a covenant marriage. The intimacy and fulfillment God intended for marriage can be experienced only if we are committed to a covenant marriage.

If all of this seems "out of reach," "too lofty to attain," "impossible for fallen man," and "out of touch" with the modern world, please move quickly to reading chapter 3.

CHAPTER THREE

COVENANT MARRIAGES: DREAM OR REALITY?

- Covenant marriages are initiated for the benefit of one's spouse.
- Covenant marriages require unconditional promises.
- Covenant marriages are based on steadfast love.
- Covenant marriages view commitments as permanent.
- Covenant marriages require confronting and forgiving.

If you have read chapters 1 and 2, it will be obvious that covenant marriage is not the typical marriage in the Western world. Most couples, even Christians, have a contractual relationship. This is one of the reasons the divorce rate among Christians has ascended in the past decade. Must we therefore conclude that the biblical ideal of a covenant marriage is outdated, beyond the grasp of modern man, a dream that exists in man's memory but simply produces guilt feelings when one seeks to apply it in the modern world?

Finding the Answer

I must confess that there was a time in my own marriage when I felt that such a covenant marriage was impossible. In my frustration, I was fast moving to the conclusion that I had two equally painful options: stay in my marriage and be miserable the rest of my life or get out, hope that God would forgive me, and pray that somewhere, somehow, I would find a happy marriage with someone else. In desperation I said to God, "I don't know what else to do. I've done everything I know to make this marriage work. I don't know where to go from here." At the time of my desperate plea I was in graduate school in seminary, preparing to be a minister. I said to God, "This isn't going to work. There is no way I can stand before people and preach your Word and be this miserable at home."

I did not hear an audible voice, but as clearly as I have ever heard anything, these are the words that penetrated my frustrated mind: *"Why don't you read the life of Jesus?"* "Read the life of Jesus?" I responded. "I am in seminary. I have read the life of Jesus many times." But the thought persisted: *"Why don't you read the life of Jesus."* So I responded, "Fine, I'll read the life of Jesus," and I added these words, "If I've missed anything, please show me."

By this time in my academic career, I had completed twenty-seven hours of Greek, so I reasoned, "I'll read the life of Jesus in Greek." So I worked my way through Matthew, Mark, Luke, and John in the Greek New Testament. What I discovered I could have discovered in any English translation. I don't know how I'd missed it all those earlier years.

I was already convinced that Jesus was the greatest leader the world has ever known. Many non-Christians will agree that no one has impacted the course of human history as did Jesus of Nazareth. But when I examined his leadership style, I did not find him making selfish demands upon his followers. Instead, I found him with a basin of water, a towel about his waist, washing the feet of his followers. And lest his actions be misunderstood, when he finished the humiliating task, he arose and explained his actions: "Do you know what I have done for you? You call Me Teacher and Lord. This is well said, for I am. So if I, your Lord and Teacher, have washed your feet, you also ought to wash one another's feet. For I have given you an example that you also should do just as I have done for you. I assure you: A slave is not greater than his master, and a messenger is not greater than the one who sent him. If you know these things, you are blessed if you do them" (John 13:12–17).

I don't know how you respond to that, but at the time I was reading those verses, the idea of washing feet did not appeal to me. In fact, I couldn't think of anything I'd rather do less. Think about it. Washing feet. But when it finally dawned on me that what Jesus was teaching was the attitude of servanthood, I realized that I had gone about my marriage in exactly the opposite way. I had made demands of my wife. I had expected her to make me happy. I realized that I was a totally secular man parading as a minister. In my desperation, I cried out, "Oh, God, I want to be like Jesus." That prayer was my first step toward a covenant marriage.

Applying the Principle of Servanthood

I'll tell you the questions that helped make the principle of servanthood practical in my marriage. When I was willing to ask these questions, my marriage began to change. The questions are: How can I help you? How can I make your life easier? How can I be a better husband to you?

When I was willing to ask those questions, do you know what I discovered? My wife was willing to give me an answer. Oh yes, she had ideas on how I could be a better husband. When I let her teach me how I could serve her, our marriage began to change. Not overnight—the pain had been there too long. But change did occur.

About two months into this new approach, I came home one evening and my wife had cooked my favorite meal. I hadn't asked for it; I had stopped asking because my requests were always interpreted as commands. But there it was—roast beef with potatoes, carrots, and onions. I was overcome, not only with the aroma but also with the awareness that she had done it without prompting from me. So I continued asking my questions and following her suggestions. I was making progress in learning the art of service. And little by little, she began to do some of the things I had berated her about in the earlier years.

About four months into this new approach to marriage, I first had the thought, *You know, maybe I could have positive feelings for her again.* I hadn't had warm feelings for a long time. My feelings were those of hurt, anger, and bitterness. I was angry at God, angry at myself, and angry with my wife for a long time. I was mad at God because I reasoned, "Before I got married, I asked you, 'Don't let me marry her if she is not the right one,' and you let me do it.'" I was mad at God for getting me into the mess. I was mad at myself because I had reasoned, "How could I, with all of my education, be so stupid as to marry a woman I can't get along with? How did I let this happen?" I was angry at her in those early years because I had reasoned, "Look, I know how to have a good marriage. Listen to me and we'll have one, and you didn't listen to me." In other words, I was an angry man before I read the life of Jesus. But four months into following Jesus, I began to sense love feelings for my wife again. About six months into this new relationship, I looked at her and had the thought, *I wouldn't mind touching her again if I thought she would let me.* I wasn't about to ask, but I had the thought, *I wouldn't mind if she wouldn't mind.*

At that juncture I knew our marriage was going to make it. We have now been walking this road for a long time. Throughout the years I have reached out to her, discovering and meeting her needs to the best of my ability. And she, in turn, has devoted her life to knowing and loving me. What has happened in our marriage is nothing short of miraculous. I'm convinced that this is the kind of marriage God intended his children to have.

In a covenant marriage, husbands and wives are both winners. In all the early years of our marriage, we were both losers. I shot her and she shot me. We both went away wounded, and came back for the next fight. When I truly became a follower of Jesus and she reciprocated, our marriage became a mutual aid society. I genuinely believe that my wife has accomplished much more in life because I have been there as her chief cheerleader and encourager. I know for certain that I would never have accomplished what I have accomplished with my life had she not been there to encourage and support me in my efforts. This, I believe, is God's plan for marriage: two people giving their lives away to each other, understanding that the ultimate goal in life is not simply to have a good marriage, but that if married, God intends us to be his encourager to each other so that together each of us will accomplish more for his kingdom than we would ever have accomplished alone.

Am I dreaming? Then let me dream on. I am reminded of the story of the street preacher who was proclaiming the love of God and calling man to repentance. A heckler walked by and said, "Shut up, old man. You're just a dreamer." In a few moments, the twelve-year-old daughter of the street preacher tapped the heckler on the shoulder, pulled him aside, and said, "Mister, I don't know who you are, but I want to tell you that that's my father who is preaching. He used to be addicted to alcohol. He would come home and steal my clothes and sell them to satisfy his cravings. But when God saved him, he got a job, started working, and began buying my clothes and shoes and school books. He never drank another drop of alcohol. Now, in all of his spare time, he tells people what God has done in his life. So, Mister, if my daddy is dreaming, don't wake him up. Please don't wake him up."

Yes, I have a dream, but I believe that dream can be a reality. I dream of a day when thousands of Christian husbands will "read the life of Jesus" and discover the key to having a covenant marriage. I believe that is God's will.

A Personal Covenant with God

Everything begins by focusing on our covenant relationship with God. Zachariah, the father of John the Baptist, was keenly aware of the covenant God made with Israel when he said, "He has raised up a horn of salvation for us in the house of His servant David. . . . He has dealt mercifully with our fathers and remembered His holy covenant—the oath that He swore to our father Abraham. He has granted us that, having been rescued from our enemies' clutches, we might serve Him without fear in holiness and righteousness in His presence all our days" (Luke 1:69, 72–75).

The Old Testament covenant had included the sacrifice of animals and the sprinkling of blood as atonements for man's sins. Through the years, many had offered such sacrifices as evidence that they were in covenant relationship with God. When Jesus instituted the Lord's Supper, he said, "This is My blood of the covenant, which is shed for many" (Mark 14:24). Thus, his sacrifice on the cross was the ultimate sacrifice for sins. Now, all who are willing to enter into the covenant relationship with God may do so by accepting his sacrifice. When we accept Jesus as our Savior, we are saying, "Yes, I will accept God's covenant promise of forgiveness and eternal life." The Lord's Supper is a symbol of our trust in Christ's death for our salvation.

Baptism is another symbol of our salvation, but there is no salvation through a symbol. Even our faith does not give us merit with God. Faith is our response to God's offer of covenant grace. He has covenanted to give us an eternal relationship with him. We enter into covenant with God when we place our faith in Jesus Christ. The essence of all God's covenants throughout history can be summarized in the statement, "I will be your God and you will be my people." Paul speaks of this covenant relationship when he says, "He redeemed us in order that the blessing given to Abraham might come to the Gentiles through Christ Jesus, so that by faith we might receive the promise of the Spirit" (Gal. 3:14 NIV). When we accept Christ as our Savior, the Holy Spirit comes to live in us. We experience a relationship with God that grows through the years and extends through eternity. All of this occurs because of God's covenant with us. This is the first step in becoming a follower of Jesus.

When one looks at the characteristics of a covenant marriage, it does indeed seem to be "otherworldly." It is unnatural in the sense that we are all self-centered, so to expect us to focus on the well-being of someone else is totally abnormal. I, for one, am fully willing to admit that apart from the work of Christ and the ministry of the Holy Spirit in my life, I am in fact self-centered and will never overcome that malady. Yet in Christ I have a new nature, and that nature motivates me to look out for the interests of others. In fact, that is the clear challenge to husbands in Ephesians 5:25, when we are asked not only to love our wives but we are given the illustration of Christ who "gave Himself for [the church]." His model is clearly the example for us. There is no question that this is God's expectation. Therefore, as Christians, we must not accept the cultural norm as our standard. Rather, we must recognize that in Christ we have an ability to transcend a strong pull of selfishness and self-centered living and to give ourselves to our wives.

Is steadfast love an impossibility in daily married life? Without the help of God, I believe the answer is yes. As Christians, however, we have the help of God. Paul reminds us that "God's love has been poured out in our hearts through the Holy Spirit who was given to us" (Rom. 5:5). The steadfast love of God is available to every Christian. Here again, the Christian has an advantage. The non-Christian is left to whatever positive regard he/she can stir up in his/her own heart. The Christian has the ability to receive the love of God and to dispense it to others. We can be God's channel for loving our spouse.

Occasionally I meet a person who has focused on the negative aspects of his spouse for so long that he has difficulty seeing the positive aspects. He asks, "How can I express positive regard for my spouse when I see no positive traits?" The answer is to follow the example of God himself: "But God proves His own love for us in that while we were still sinners Christ died for us!" (Rom. 5:8). God did not wait until we were lovely before he loved us. Though the Scriptures say that God cannot "countenance" sin—that he hates sin—even while we were sinners, God still loved us.

"That's fine for God," some will say, "but how about me?" Again, I would return to the truth stated in Romans 5:5: "God's love has been poured out in our hearts through the Holy Spirit." God's ability to love unlovely people is available to us. If we will open our hearts to God's love and in essence say to him, "Lord, you know the person with whom I live; you know that I have great difficulty in seeing anything positive about him; but I know that you love him. I want to be your channel for loving him. Use my hands, my tongue, and my body to express your love." We can have God's help and become lovers of what we perceive to be unlovely.

Some will raise the question, "How can I continue to forgive my spouse when he/she does the same thing over and over again?" Peter raised this question: "Lord, how many times could my brother sin against me and I forgive him? As many as seven times?" Jesus answered, "I tell you, not as many as seven . . . but 70 times seven" (Matt. 18:21–22). Obviously, there is room to question one's sincerity if he commits the same failure that often, but Jesus indicates that we do not have the ability to judge another's sincerity. Jesus says that if they confess, we are to forgive. The lasting answer to such repeated offenses lies in trying to discover why the person continues to fail in the same area. Usually there are emotional reasons why a person continues to fail. Finding the answer may require counseling; it may require openness with Christian friends or a pastor; it may even require "tough love"—sometimes the most powerful expression of love—as a way of motivating the spouse to deal with the problem in a responsible manner. But certainly the root of the problem needs to be dealt with if there is to be a lasting answer.

≥ ≥ ≥

The standards for a covenant marriage are indeed beyond human ability; however, as Christians, we have divine help available. In his power we can forgive as he forgives and love as he loves. Covenant marriage does not depend on human perfection—it is based on steadfast love worked out in our hearts by the Holy Spirit giving us the ability to give and forgive. An intimate relationship with God is the key to turning dreams into realities.

Working from the foundation of our intimate relationship with God, we next focus on establishing intimacy with our spouse. In chapter 4 we will explore the reasons why intimacy is necessary in a covenant marriage.

CHAPTER FOUR

WHAT'S SO IMPORTANT ABOUT INTIMACY?

Henry was a loyal deacon who seldom missed a meeting and was usually jovial and positive. Tonight, however, I noticed that he came to the meeting late and didn't have much to say. After the meeting was over, he lingered while the others scattered. "How are things going, Henry?" I asked. He looked at the floor and said, "I'm not sure I'll ever understand women." "What makes you say that?" I inquired. "My wife says that she thinks we need more intimacy in our marriage. She says that we are not close like we used to be. I hate to admit it, but I don't know what she is talking about. I thought we had a good marriage, but she seems very unhappy lately. I really don't know what to do about it."

Henry is not alone in his lack of understanding of intimacy. Many husbands and wives have heard the word *intimacy* but have little understanding of what it means. So, let me ask the questions: What is intimacy? Why is it so important in a covenant marriage? I would like to suggest that the whole idea originated with God. Early on, God looked at Adam and said, "It is not good for the man to be alone" (Gen. 2:18). The word translated *alone* is a Hebrew word that literally means "cut off." It is the same Hebrew word that you would use to speak of cutting off your hand. It would not be good for the hand to be alone, wouldn't you agree? God said that it is not good for man to be alone—cut off. God was identifying what we have come to recognize as one of our society's deepest emotional problems. Sociologists call it the problem of alienation; most of us call it the problem of loneliness.

A number of years ago, I started the single adult ministry at our church. We presently have more than six hundred single adults involved in this ministry. Do you know the most common complaint of single adults? "I am so lonely." There is something about our psychological, spiritual, and physical makeup that cries out for intimacy with another. It is not normal for a person to live in isolation.

God's answer to Adam's aloneness was the creation of Eve and the institution of marriage. God said, "I will make him a helper suitable for him. . . . and they will become one flesh" (Gen. 2:18, 24). The Hebrew word for *one* is the same Hebrew word used in Deuteronomy 6:4: "Hear, O Israel: the LORD our God, the LORD is one." This word speaks of a unity made up of distinct parts. In the case of God, it is three who are one—Father, Son, and Holy Spirit—one God. In marriage, it is two who are to become one. Such oneness is at the heart of what marriage is all about. *Oneness* is a synonym for *intimacy.*

This oneness or intimacy in marriage does not mean that we lose our individuality. In the Bible we can clearly distinguish the difference between God the Father, God the Son, and God the Holy Spirit. One God is expressed in three persons. They are not identical, but they are one. We say of God that there is unity with diversity. The same is to be true of a Christian marriage. The diversity allows our freedom, our uniqueness. The unity is a picture of deep intimacy.

Have you ever been somewhere alone and experienced something— a sound, a sight, a smell—and said to yourself aloud, "Oh, I wish my mate could be here"? What motivates such a statement? It is the deep, natural desire to share life with another person with whom you have a significant relationship. Most of us will find ways to capture the moment with photographs, postcards, tape recordings, or other means so that we can later—by letter, phone call, or personal encounter—share with our spouse these experiences. Marriage was designed by God to deliver us from loneliness.

I am not suggesting that a person must be married in order to be happy. What I am suggesting is that even in singleness, people need people. In most of our churches, the single adult group is one of the most active groups in the church. The group members recognize the need to build relationships and friendships with each other. Singles, as well as married couples, want and need private time for reading, reflecting, praying, and so on, but balanced with this desire for privacy is the need for friendship and closeness with others.

God designed marriage to be the most intimate of all human relationships. We are going to share life—intellectually, socially, emotionally, spiritually, and physically—and we are going to share life to such a degree that it can be said of us, we become *one*. The degree to which a Christian couple attains intimacy in each of these areas determines the degree of satisfaction in their marriage. To the degree that a couple does not discover such intimacy, marriage will become empty. In our society, we have many married couples who are living together, but they are still alone, cut off. They are not finding the intimacy of which the Bible speaks.

It should be obvious then that intimacy encompasses all of life. In the area of intellectual intimacy, couples share with each other their thoughts, experiences, ideas, and desires. In social intimacy, they experience interaction with others together. This may include such things as symphonies, recreational activities, or Sunday school picnics in which they interact with others. In emotional intimacy, couples share feelings, emotional responses to things that are occurring in life. Spiritual intimacy involves sharing a response to the morning sermon, something that has impressed us in a personal quiet time with God, or a challenging biblical principle. Physical intimacy involves the whole area of physical touch—holding hands, kissing, embracing, and sexual intercourse. It is possible that one of these areas may be developed more fully than another. Ideally, all of them need to be developed as couples grow together.

What was Henry's wife wanting when she said, "Our marriage needs more intimacy?" I had no way of knowing without talking to his wife, but I was relatively certain that in one or more of these five areas, she did not feel a sense of oneness with Henry. Intimacy is at the very heart of marriage. Man's need for intimacy is what motivated God to create Eve and institute the marriage relationship. When intimacy is not developed in a marriage, the marriage becomes like a wilted plant longing for water. Intimacy is the rain that gives a marriage its vitality. Thus, intimacy is extremely important in a covenant marriage. That is why, in the chapters ahead, we will focus our attention on practical ways to enhance intimacy.

On the other hand, there are people like Henry who seem to be satisfied with their marriage. "I thought we had a good marriage," he said. I later discovered that Henry had never been really close to anyone. All of his relationships, including the family in which he grew up, were arm-length relationships emotionally. He had learned to live without intimacy. Having gone so long without an intimate relationship, he did not have a felt need for such closeness. In fact, Henry had very little awareness of his emotions. To speak of an emotional need or the desire for an emotional relationship was a foreign language to him.

&a &a &a

In chapter 9 we will deal with the question, "How does one get in touch with emotions?" Then in chapter 10 we will discuss ways to stimulate emotional intimacy. Before we do that, however, I want to address a more fundamental issue: How does communication relate to intimacy?

CHAPTER FIVE

COMMUNICATION: THE ROAD TO INTIMACY

When divorced couples were asked, "Why did your marriage fail?" 86 percent said, "Deficient communication." If that is true, then communication in marriage must be extremely important.

Communication involves self-revelation on the part of one individual and listening on the part of another. In its simplest form, communication is talking and listening; however, unless talking and listening are accompanied by honest, loving feedback on the part of the listener, little communication can take place. In fact, miscommunication and misunderstanding will probably be the results. In good marital communication the husband and wife each share thoughts, feelings, experiences, values, priorities, and judgments while the other listens sympathetically. Both partners share on the same open, honest level. (In later chapters we will discuss some practical ways to enhance this process.)

God's Divine Example

God's communication to man is the model for our communication with each other. The Scriptures say that God has spoken to man in many ways throughout history. He has spoken through angels, visions, dreams, nature, creation, and, supremely, through his Son, Jesus Christ. All of this is recorded in the Bible. How did the Bible come into existence? "Holy men of God spoke as they were moved by the Holy Spirit" (2 Pet. 1:21 NKJV). The result is that the Bible gives us words from God. Thus, we have the potential for knowing God because God has spoken. Yet we know there are many people who do not have a relationship with God because they have either not listened to his self-revelation or they have responded negatively and walked away to live alone. Thus, they have no relationship and no fellowship with God. There is no intimacy between them and the Creator.

On the other hand, for those who have accepted Christ, intimacy with him is a matter of degree. It is obvious that some Christians are much closer to God than other Christians. The vehicle for gaining intimacy with God as a Christian is regular communication with God. We are to listen to God as he speaks to us through his Word, and we are to respond to God with our honest thoughts, feelings, and decisions. When God speaks, we listen to him. When we speak, God listens to us. Through this process over a period of time, an individual can have a growing intimacy with the God of the universe. There is nothing in life more important than this kind of relationship with God; it enhances all of life both here and hereafter.

The same is true in a covenant marriage: communication leads to intimacy. In 1 Corinthians 2:11, Paul raises a question that every woman has asked, "Who . . . knows the thoughts of a man?" Answer? Only "the man's spirit within him" (NIV). Essentially, Paul is saying that only you know what is going on in your mind. The old saying "I can read him like a book" is simply not true. Wives, you may think you know what is going on in your husband's mind, but actually, you don't. Husbands, you know that you don't know what is going on in her mind, right? If you have been married for thirty years and you have had lots of open communication, there may be some truth to the statement, "I can read him like a book." Ultimately, however, it is never fully true. We cannot read another person's mind.

Body language is supposed to tell us about people by the way they fold their arms, cross their legs, sit, speak, or use facial expressions. It is true that we can pick up cues from a person's behavior, but we can never know what is in others' minds simply by looking at them. For example, when you observe a lady crying, you may assume that she is troubled. However, you have no idea by observation whether she is experiencing grief over the loss of a spouse or a child, whether she has just been fired from her job, or whether she has just hit her thumb with a hammer. Her tears may even be tears of joy. Only if she chooses to tell you will you know what is behind her tears.

Verbal communication is essential in order to understand what is going on inside other people. If they do not tell us their thoughts, their feelings, and their experiences, we are left to guess. Unfortunately, our guess is usually wrong, and we misunderstand them. That is why communication is an absolute necessity if we are to reach intimacy. We will never experience what God had in mind when he ordained marriage if we do not communicate with each other. As we come to understand the process of communication and learn how to overcome barriers to communication, our experience of intimacy will bring us the joy God intended.

The First Step

The remainder of this book is designed to enhance communication and intimacy. We will look at some of the reasons why 86 percent of those who divorce say that the main problem was deficient communication. But before we look at the weightier matters, let me suggest an easy step to enhance communication: Plan a daily sharing time with your spouse. Couples who have a "sit down, look at me, let's talk" time each day have a higher level of intimacy than those couples who simply talk "whenever and wherever." Couples who practice a daily sharing time will tend to talk more with each other at other times as well.

So, what do you talk about in this daily sharing time? Just keep it simple. Here is what I call the "daily minimum requirement": "Tell me three things that happened in your life today and how you feel about them." Based on a survey I conducted, my conclusion is that 50 percent of the married couples in this country do not meet this daily minimum requirement. When I share this idea with couples, someone in the group will say, "Oh, we already do that," or "I'm sure we share at least three things with each other every day." So I probe. "Great. Share with the group the three things you shared with each other today," to which they typically respond, "Oh. Well, we didn't have time to talk today; we had to come to this meeting. You know you have to rush to get here on time." I say, "Fine. Share with the group three things you shared with each other yesterday." "Well, uhh. Last night was PTA meeting, and we never have time to talk on PTA night." "Fine. Share with us the three things you shared with each other the day before yesterday." "Well. That was soccer night. We don't ever get a chance to talk on soccer night, especially when we lose." You, too, may come to the realization that you may not be meeting the daily minimum requirement.

Some couples complain, "My life is the same every day. I don't have anything to share. It is always the same routine. There is no need to share it." The fact is that none of us experiences the same thing every day. It may be true that our job is monotonous. We may do the same physical functions every day on our jobs, but all of us think different thoughts throughout the day. We have different feelings. And some things are different each day—traffic patterns vary on the way to and from work, the lunch menu is not always the same, conversations we have with people will vary from day to day along with the weather and the information we receive on the radio or television. Things are not the same every day. Perhaps we are simply using this as an excuse for not sharing with our spouses.

"But nothing important ever happens in my life," some say. Who determines what is important? Is eating lunch important? Is getting a drink of water important? Perhaps your life has not been exciting today, but it has been your life. It you want intimacy in your marriage, you must share life. If you had a boring day, let your spouse in on your day so he/she has an opportunity to respond to your boredom. If you don't self-reveal, your spouse has no way of knowing where you are emotionally, and he/she is left to guess. Often the guess will be wrong.

Every couple needs a daily time when they can look into each other's eyes, talk, and listen as they share life with each other. This kind of quality time spent daily is one of the most fundamental exercises a couple can do to enhance intimacy in a marriage relationship. Many couples go for days without such a sharing time. Each is involved in a busy schedule, and they simply communicate those things necessary for carrying on the daily routine. Emotionally, they grow further apart.

What we are talking about here is the simplest and easiest level of communication—sharing with each other some of our day-to-day events and how we feel about those events. Regular communication on this basic level builds a platform that supports communication on more intimate and sometimes difficult levels.

Couples who desire an intimate relationship must share not only some of the things they experience throughout the day but also their feelings about those events. For example, a husband comes home from work and shares with his wife that he had a conversation with his supervisor and was informed that he is to receive a pay raise. The wife asks, "How do you feel about that, darling?" He may respond, "Elated! I didn't expect a raise until the first of the year." On the other hand, he may say, "Do you want to know the truth? I feel disappointed. The raise should have been twice as much as it was." Whichever way he responds, the wife now knows her husband better. Because he has shared a little of his emotional life, she can enter his world and have a greater sense of emotional intimacy. If he does not share his feelings verbally, she may detect something of his emotional response by his physical behavior, but the communication is much clearer when he verbalizes his feelings to her. We are emotional creatures, and we have emotional responses to the things that happen to us throughout the day. If we are going to build intimacy in marriage, we must learn to share some of our emotions.

For many couples, daily communication consists of the following scenario: Husband walks into the house. Wife walks into the house. Wife says to husband, "How did things go today, dear?" He responds, "Fine," as he turns on the TV to watch the evening news, or he heads for the backyard to mow the grass. Though they have been apart for eight to ten hours, cut off from each other, he summarizes their time apart with one word—*fine*. And the husband wonders why his wife complains that they no longer have intimacy in their marriage! One word is not an adequate summary of ten hours apart. We must learn to have daily communication times.

ða ða ða

Good communication is the road to intimacy. Poor communication leads couples down dead-end streets and through numerous detours. In the following chapters, it is my objective to provide a road map to help you reach the destination of an intimate covenant marriage through productive communication. We begin, in chapter 6, by looking at some unhealthy patterns of communication. Good communication requires that we identify and eliminate the unhealthy and then find new ways of communicating that foster understanding and intimacy.

CHAPTER SIX

UNHEALTHY PATTERNS OF COMMUNICATION

Communication is not like an event we attend and then it is over. Communication is more like the process of breathing; without it, we do not continue. Nor is intimacy something we gain and retain forever. We do not obtain intimacy and put it in a safe deposit box. It is fluid and directly related to the quality of communication between the couple.

Communication is not enough. It must be healthy communication if we are going to experience intimacy. Just as breathing toxic fumes can lead to death, so unhealthy communication patterns can actually destroy intimacy. In our efforts to maintain our emotional stability, we develop patterns of communication. These patterns are learned ways of responding to and communicating with our spouses. After awhile, we are not even aware of our communication patterns; we are simply doing what comes natural to us.

Some of our communication patterns are positive, leading us to intimacy in marriage. But many communication patterns are negative, leading couples apart rather than together. Some couples genuinely desire intimacy, but unknown to them, their communication patterns lead them farther and farther apart. Before we can correct unhealthy communication patterns, we must first identify them. Over the years, those who study marriage have discovered common patterns that are detrimental to marital intimacy. These patterns are passed from parent to child, and it is not uncommon to see these unhealthy patterns repeated generation after generation. The good news is that these patterns can be broken by any couple who is willing to examine their patterns and make needed corrections.

The Four "Fowls"

By looking at the communication patterns of our parents, we can often more easily identify our own. In this chapter, we will identify four unhealthy patterns of communication. Reflect on the communication pattern of your parents and see whether you identify any of these patterns in their marriage. Then look at your own marriage and see whether your pattern is the same or different. If different, in what way is it different? Almost all of these unhealthy patterns develop from a need to maintain emotional stability, to feel good about ourselves. But when these patterns are negative, they are detrimental to marital intimacy. These unhealthy patterns can be remembered when compared to four fowls: the dove, the hawk, the owl, and the ostrich.

Dove: "I Want Peace at Any Price"

In this pattern, one partner placates the other in order to avoid his/her wrath. Typical dove statements are, "That's fine with me," or "Whatever makes you happy makes me happy." The dove is always trying to please the other person, often apologizing, even for little things that may have stimulated the anger of the spouse. The dove will almost never disagree with his/her spouse, no matter how they feel.

Several years ago, I was counseling a man whose wife had left him after twenty-five years of marriage. When I asked him, "What happened in your marriage?" his response was, "I have been analyzing it, and I think I have figured it out. In the early stages of our marriage, my wife did many things that irritated me. But as you know, I am a peacemaker. I don't like conflict, and as you also know, my wife has a fiery personality. If I disagreed with her or mentioned some irritation to her, she would explode. Therefore, to avoid the explosion, I simply started staying away from her. When I did talk to her, I communicated that whatever she did, whatever she said, and whatever she wanted was fine with me, even though inside I strongly resented it.

"Looking back on it, I realize that I started working longer hours. When I was at home, I began spending more time with my computer and less time with her. I was not fully aware of what I was doing, but in retrospect, I see that I walked farther and farther away from her emotionally to avoid the conflicts. I got involved in my job and in ministry at the church. She got involved in her job and her ministry, and we grew farther and farther apart. We didn't have arguments, but after awhile, we didn't have a relationship either. Finally, I guess she just decided that there had to be more to life than what we were experiencing, and she left me to find it."

In his efforts to avoid conflict and maintain his own sense of emotional stability and safety, he had relinquished all possibility of intimacy. This is a classic example of what happens to those who emulate the dove. Peace at any price carries a high price tag indeed.

Hawk: "It's Your Fault"

The hawk blames his/her spouse for everything. The blamer is the boss, the dictator, the one in charge who never does wrong. Typical hawk statements are, "You never do anything right. You always botch it up. I don't understand how you could be so stupid. If it weren't for you, everything would be fine."

Hawks appear to be strong and belligerent people. In reality, they are weak emotionally. They feel bad about themselves, but when they put someone else down or get someone to obey them, they feel better about themselves. Thus, their pattern of faultfinding has been developed to meet their own emotional weakness. How the other spouse responds to the hawk's faultfinding depends upon their own emotional pattern. If they happen to struggle with their own self-esteem, they may simply believe what the hawk says and accept it as truth. If, on the other hand, they feel good about themselves and have a positive self-image, they may fight, and the relationship may be characterized by periodic verbal battles.

Brad was a husband who had never maintained steady employment. His pattern for several years before marriage was part-time jobs, none of which lasted more than six months. He did not own a car when they got married, and he still lived with his parents. After marriage, he constantly blamed his wife for everything. It was her fault that he ran out of gas while driving the car she owned when they got married. It was her fault that the electric company turned off the power when the bill was not paid, and it was her fault when his clothes were not washed in spite of the fact that they lived seven blocks from a washing machine and he was gone in the car all day Saturday. "She should have walked to the laundromat" was his reasoning.

His wife, Madelyn, who suffered from low self-esteem, vacillated between two patterns of response for years. She would simply accept his judgments for awhile, and then when the resentment built to a certain level, she would leave him for three or four weeks. When her loneliness eventually overwhelmed her, she would come back, and the cycle would start again. Obviously, there was little intimacy in their marriage. Sex? Yes, from time to time. Intimacy? No.

All of us know that no one can be wrong all the time while the other is always right. However, in this pattern of communication, the facts are considered unimportant. Hawks seldom wait for an answer to their accusations. The important thing to them is not what the other person thinks but their own judgment. It reminds me of Proverbs 18:2: "A fool does not delight in understanding, but only wants to show off his opinions."

Owl: "Let's Be Reasonable"

The owl is Mr. or Mrs. Calm, Cool, and Collected. This person shows no feelings; he says the right words; he reveals no emotional reaction when his spouse disagrees with him. He is more like a computer than a person. Owls give you logical answers to every question. He will calmly explain anything about which you have a question. He will make it sound so reasonable that you will wonder how anyone could have thought otherwise. An owl usually thinks of himself as being a reasonable and intelligent person. He prides himself on not showing emotion; and when the other person shows emotion, he calmly sits until the storm is over and then proceeds with his reasoning.

A wife once said to me, "My husband drives me crazy being so reasonable. He takes hours explaining things to me as though I am a two-year-old who knows nothing. He never gets upset with me. He lets me speak, but he hears nothing I say. Consequently, most of the time I don't even say anything. It does no good." Do you think this lady is drawn to intimacy with her husband? Who wants to make love with a computer? This communication pattern does not lead to intimacy on any level.

What is going on inside the owl will vary from person to person, but commonly this individual feels vulnerable inside. Her efforts at being ultrareasonable are designed primarily to convince herself of her worth and of her intellectual abilities. It is a compensation for feelings of inadequacy about herself. If she can control her feelings, if she can reason her way through something, she feels emotionally secure. Thus, the pattern serves an emotional function for her, but it is an unhealthy function in the marriage relationship.

Ostrich: "Ignore It and It Will Go Away"

The ostrich's pattern of communicating basically ignores the other person's actions and comments, especially if he finds them disagreeable. The ostrich seldom responds directly to what the other person says. He doesn't respond negatively; he simply doesn't respond. He changes the subject and moves on to something totally unrelated to what the spouse just said. The ostrich is an activist. If he is a talker, he will rattle on and on about nothing related to anything. If he is a doer rather than a talker, then he will constantly be involved in activity, but most of the activities will not be related to each other. If you ask a question about what he is doing, you will not get a direct response because he is not sure how what he is doing fits in with anything else.

The ostrich often develops a sing-song approach to talking. Often the inflection of his voice is out of tune with his words. You can interrupt him, make your own comments, and he will start talking again unrelated to what you have just said or what he was saying beforehand. His conversation goes in all directions and seldom reaches any conclusions.

A husband once said to me about his wife, "I cannot carry on a conversation with her. She talks on and on and says absolutely nothing. If I try to respond to something she is saying or try to ask a question, she ignores the question or asks me a question totally unrelated to what I asked her. I can never discuss issues with her because she won't stay on the subject. She may chase ten rabbits in one conversation and never get back on the original trail." Do you sense the frustration of this husband? He is not certain in his own mind whether she simply does not want to talk to him or does not have the ability. At any rate, he knows that they do not have an intimate relationship.

For the most part, those who follow the communication pattern of the ostrich think of themselves as "not fitting in." There is no place for them in the world. Typically, this perception about themselves developed in childhood and has followed them into adult relationships. Their speech and behavior pattern simply reflect this inner perception. It is obvious that such a pattern is unhealthy in trying to develop an intimate marriage relationship.

Sometimes the ostrich refuses to admit or discuss problems because they fear getting into arguments. Arguments are extremely unsettling to this person. At all costs, they wish to avoid them. They really believe that if you simply ignore it, it will go away. What they do not realize is that the problem never goes away; it simply sits as a barrier to marital intimacy.

The four communication patterns we have discussed are unhealthy for marital intimacy. They will be detrimental to intellectual, emotional, social, spiritual, and physical intimacy in marriage. Unfortunately, instead of trying to find answers to these unhealthy patterns, many Christians look for biblical reasons for continuing these patterns. For example, the dove will quote verses such as Romans 12:18: "If possible, on your part, live at peace with everyone," or, 1 Corinthians 13:5, which indicates that love "is not selfish; is not provoked; does not keep a record of wrongs."

The hawk will be attracted to the statement in Psalms that implores God to wipe out his enemies and also to the New Testament passages in which Jesus overthrew the tables of the money changers (Matt. 21:12–13). The owl will quote Isaiah 1:18: "'Come now, let us reason together,' says the LORD." The ostrich will follow Jonah's line of reasoning when he said to God, "'O LORD, is this not what I said when I was still at home? That is why I was so quick to flee to Tarshish. I knew that you are a gracious and compassionate God, slow to anger and abounding in love, a God who relents from sending calamity'" (Jonah 4:2–3). His deduction? "I should have stayed at home." This person thus concludes that everything will work out anyway, so why should I be concerned about anything. Using Scripture to justify our own unhealthy patterns of communication reminds me of the words of Peter when he spoke of twisting Scripture to meet our own needs (2 Pet. 3:16).

Establishing Healthy Patterns

How does a couple go about correcting these unhealthy patterns? Consider the following ideas. First, we must identify the pattern. Obviously we cannot change an unhealthy pattern until we are aware of it. I noted earlier that you might begin by identifying these patterns in your parents and then looking for them in your own marriage.

Secondly, admit that this pattern is detrimental to your own marital intimacy. Stand in front of the mirror and say, "I am an owl. This is really the way I communicate to my spouse, and it is detrimental to our marital intimacy." Saying it to yourself will make it easier for you to admit it to your spouse.

Decide that you want to see the pattern changed. Most positive changes in our lives happen because we decide that they will happen. God gave us tremendous power when he gave us a will. Throughout the Bible there is a strong emphasis upon human choice. Healthy communication is largely dependent upon choice. When you decide to change an unhealthy pattern, you will have the help of the Holy Spirit. He is ever present to empower us to break destructive patterns.

Replace old patterns with new patterns of communication. This was the emphasis in Paul's epistles when he spoke of putting off the old man and putting on the new man (Eph. 4:22–24). In the following pages you will discover numerous positive patterns of communication. Working these into the fabric of your marriage will help you break the destructive patterns of the past.

Admit failure when you revert to the old pattern. No communication pattern will be changed overnight. You will have relapses into the old unhealthy way of communicating. A relapse does not mean failure; it is the normal part of changing any habitual action.

A periodic checkup with your spouse will be helpful. Seek their honest feedback. Habits and patterns, by their nature, tend to be tenacious. Periodically we need to discuss our progress with each other. Saying to your spouse, "Be honest with me. Have I slipped back into my old pattern this week?" opens the door for your spouse to be honest. If these checkup sessions are held in a loving, caring context, they can be extremely valuable.

    èa èa èa

You need not continue in unhealthy communication patterns learned from your parents and fostered by your own personality. With the help of God, you can "put off" the old and "put on" new and healthy patterns of talking and listening to your spouse. Now let's turn our attention to understanding the dynamics of healthy communication. We begin by looking at five levels of communication.

CHAPTER SEVEN

FIVE LEVELS
OF COMMUNICATION

Just as it is helpful to identify certain communication patterns, it is also helpful to understand that various levels of communication exist. All communication is not equal in value. Some levels of communication foster greater intimacy than others. We will certainly communicate on all five levels, but in a marriage relationship we desire to spend more and more time on the higher levels. In this chapter, we discuss five levels of communication so that you will be able to identify the level you are on in any conversation. With this information, you will be able to heighten the level of your communication with your spouse and thus build greater intimacy. Picture the five levels as five ascending steps that lead to a large platform where there will be free and open communication.

Level 1: Hallway Talk—"Fine, how are you?"

Level 1 is what we experience as we walk down the hallways at work or church. Some time ago, I was walking down the hallway of the church where I serve and noticed in the distance a janitor at work. As I approached, I did not speak to him. I said nothing, but when I got within eight feet of him, he looked up and said, "Fine. How are you?" to which I responded, "Fine," and walked on. I realized as I passed him that I had not initiated the conversation. I had not asked, "How are you?" His response was so learned and so automatic that it simply took an approaching human to elicit his automatic response. Obviously, this level of communication is shallow, and yet all of us communicate a great deal on this level. If the hallway is long, you can solicit half a dozen "Fine. How are you?" responses before you get to the elevator.

Level 1 involves surface talk—the nice, polite things we say to one another throughout the day, the expected things. We give little thought to these statements; they are almost rote because we have said them so often in the past, and we will say them in the future. We have learned them from childhood; they are part of our culture. We give little, if any, thought to what the words mean. If we reflect on what we are saying, we usually are sincere. The fact is, however, that normally we do not reflect on what we are saying on this level. "Have a good day." "I love you." "Be careful." "See you later." "Goodnight." "Take care." These and scores of other statements that we make each day are spoken on the first step of the communication stairway.

Such statements are not to be thought of as totally useless; they are positive and they do acknowledge the other person's presence. If you doubt their value, abstain from saying these things and see what response you get. Or, worse yet, replace one of these positive statements with a negative statement. For example instead of saying "Be careful," say "I hope you have a wreck on the way to work." Observe how that affects the behavior of your spouse. These positive "Fine, how are you?" statements are not without value. There are a few couples for whom even this level of communication would be an improvement, for they walk in and out of each other's lives daily and say nothing. Even a "Good morning" would be a welcomed word to these couples.

Much of our communication at public gatherings is on this first level. Bryan walks up to Nathan and says, "Great to see you, Nathan. How are you?" to which Nathan responds, "Fine. How's your family?"

Bryan continues, "Just fine, thank you. How's yours?" Nathan replies, "Great. Just great. Everybody is just fine." The fact is that Nathan's wife has been sick with a cold for three weeks, and last week they discovered that their youngest daughter has a learning disability. Bryan's mother passed away a month ago, and his wife told him last night that if things don't change, she is leaving. But neither Bryan nor Nathan feels free to share these things; or maybe this is not the time or the place. After all, the only answer anyone expects is "Fine. How are you?"

Some people never get beyond this first level of communication. Several years ago a young wife whose husband is a pilot said to me, "My husband is gone three days and home three days. That is his work schedule. He comes home after three days away, and I say to him, 'How did things go, dear?' He says, 'Fine.' Three days and all I get is 'Fine,'" she screamed. His one-word summary of three days away is not enough to make her feel close to him. Some couples go days speaking only on this level. They should not be surprised by the lack of intimacy in their relationship.

Level 2: Reporter Talk—"Just give me the facts."

Conversation on level 2 involves only the facts: who, what, when, and where. You tell each other what you have seen and heard, when and where it took place, but you share nothing of your opinions about the events. For example, a wife says to her husband, "I talked to Myra this morning, and she told me that Paul has been sick for six days. The doctor recommends that he go to the hospital Friday for tests." Her husband responds, "Hmm." Myra continues, "She said that he had been complaining of pain in his lower back, and after six days of bed rest, he doesn't seem to be any better." To which the husband responds, "Hmm." Then the wife continues reporting additional facts or changes the subject, or perhaps her husband changes the subject and asks, "Did Junior find the dog?" The wife responds, "Yes. One of the neighbors had him locked in their backyard and didn't know that he belonged to us. Junior heard him barking this afternoon and went to rescue him." The husband walks out the door to mow the grass.

On this level of communication we are simply sharing factual material but volunteering nothing of ourselves and asking nothing of others—no opinions about what we think about the subject, no expressions about how we feel. We do not express our thoughts or reactions to the information we hear.

Reporter talk may involve vast areas of life: what time the musical starts at church, where we will meet for lunch, how much it will cost to get the yard seeded, when we are celebrating your mother's birthday, when Jason will be home from college. This is the kind of information that is shared on level 2.

I am not suggesting that this level of communication is unimportant; the success of much of life is dependent upon this kind of communication. Many couples have ended up at different restaurants because of lack of clarity in communicating at this level. I once ended up at the wrong church to perform a wedding because I didn't get my facts straight. When I finally got to the right church, the organist had played all of her music twice, and the guests were wondering if the groom had changed his mind.

Factual information is important. Without it, life would be difficult. The point is, however, that a couple with a poor marriage relationship can usually talk on this level. In fact, hundreds of marriages exist on this level. They simply share with each other the facts that are necessary to carry on daily life, but their relationship doesn't go beyond that. Some couples who communicate regularly on level 2 think that they really have good communication. In reality, little intellectual, emotional, spiritual, or physical intimacy is built on this level of communication.

Level 3: Intellectual Talk—"Do you know what I think?"

Level 3 goes beyond the sharing of factual information. We are now sharing our opinions, interpretations, or judgments about the matter. We are letting another person in on how we are processing the factual information in our minds. The following statements illustrate level 3 communication: "I think we should buy a boat with the money we got back from our tax refund." "I think the church should give more money to foreign missions." "I wish we could spend a weekend together in the mountains soon." "If Randy doesn't bring his grades up, I don't think we should buy him a car." Such statements definitely reflect a higher level of communication.

How might the husband's conversation with his wife about Paul's illness move from level 2 to level 3? Consider the following. The husband might respond by saying, "Do you know what I think? I think Paul should see a chiropractor. Do you remember last year when I had that back problem and the doctor told me that I needed to be in traction for three days? I went to the chiropractor, and with a thirty-minute treatment, I was well. I really think Paul needs to see a chiropractor."

In this statement, the husband reveals something of himself. Based on past experience, he shares with his wife his judgment on Paul's condition. If his wife responds by saying, "I don't know. I am not sure that this is the answer for him. You remember Jeff? He went to the chiropractor for six months, and he was worse when he got through than when he started. I am not sure that is the answer." In sharing such a statement, his wife also takes another step up the stairway of communication by sharing her ideas and thoughts on the subject.

Obviously the possibility of conflict or differences is much more likely on level 3 than on levels 1 or 2. If the husband struggles with his own self-esteem, if he is not sure of himself emotionally, he may drop the conversation at this point because he does not want to deal with his wife's opposition to his idea. If he has a different personality, he may pursue the matter and lecture her on the value of going to the chiropractor.

Typically when people talk on this level, they watch for the response of the other person. If the other person responds positively to their ideas, they continue talking and asking questions of each other. If the other person, however, has a negative response that is expressed in words or facial expressions (a frown, raised eyebrows, narrowed eyes, a yawn), then the other person may quickly bring the conversation to a close and retreat to a safer subject. Some couples spend little time on level 3 because they don't like to have their ideas challenged or questioned. Emotionally they are threatened; therefore, they retreat to levels 1 or 2 and may never move to level 4.

A necessity for communication growth is giving each other the freedom to think differently. It is not necessary that a couple agree on every subject. It is perfectly legitimate for a husband to have one concept of the value of chiropractors and his wife to have another perception. Such differences need not affect their intimacy. But when one tries to force the other to agree with his opinions, then intimacy evaporates and argument or silence prevails.

Level 4: Emotional Talk—"Let me tell you how I feel."

On level 4 we share our emotions and how we feel about things. "I feel hurt, disappointed, angry, happy, sad, excited, bored, unloved, romantic, or lonely." These are the kinds of feeling words we use on this level. For most people, sharing feelings is more difficult than sharing thoughts. Our feelings are more private. We often sit in a group and share our thoughts freely with the group without ever revealing what we feel about what is going on in the group. In fact, our expressed thoughts may often camouflage our feelings. For example, the husband may say to the wife, "I thought the pastor's sermon was too long." Inside, he may be feeling angry at the pastor because the sermon stimulated guilt over his failures. His statement to his wife focuses on time, but his emotions are not related to the time; they are related to the content.

The distance between level 3 and level 4 may be a giant step. If I share my feelings and you don't like my feelings, you may be hurt or disappointed in me, or you may get angry with me. I may then have great difficulty coping with your rejection or anger; therefore, I may be reluctant to share my feelings again. We risk much more when we communicate on this level, but we also have the potential for entering a higher level of intimacy.

What we feel about something most vividly communicates our uniqueness as a person. No one feels exactly as I feel about a given subject. Even if we come to the same conclusion, we do not feel the same way about it. For example, a husband and wife may agree that they should join a certain church. Even though both of them may be 100 percent in favor of doing this, they will still have different feelings about the decision based on their personal histories. The husband may totally agree that this is the right thing to do, but inside he may fear his mother's response or he may feel that he is betraying his grandfather, who was a pastor in another denomination. Or he may wonder how his boss, who belongs to still another denomination, will respond. Or he may hope that the pastor will not emphasize tithing, for he really doesn't feel that he can afford to tithe. Or he may feel excited about the possibility of teaching a youth Sunday school class because he loves teenagers. Or he may hope that no one will discover him, that he can sit quietly in the pew for the next year. The wife, on the other hand, will have another set of emotions based on her history and her personality. We are all unique individuals. When we share our feelings, we share ourselves. Thus in a marriage, when we communicate on this level, we have the potential of enhancing marital intimacy.

Many couples seldom communicate on this level because they fear that their emotions will not be accepted. A wife says to her husband, "I really have been feeling depressed for the last few days," to which the husband responds, "Depressed? Woman, how could you feel depressed with all the things you have?" Chances are the conversation is over, and the wife will be reluctant to share her feelings from that point on. When we repress our feelings, our spouse is left to imagine what is going on inside of us.

Couples often misread each other and develop misunderstandings. In the earlier conversation concerning the chiropractor, let's imagine that the husband says to his wife, "You know, dear, I'm beginning to feel that whatever I think on a subject, you are automatically going to think the opposite. If I believe in chiropractors, you hate chiropractors. If I think that going to the PTA is a waste of time, you think it is the greatest thing in the world. I feel that you just don't like me and that this is the way you communicate it. Disagreeing with everything I say is your way of communicating that you don't like me."

To such an open statement his wife may immediately become defensive and, depending on her personality, either start to cry and withdraw or verbally express her anger toward him by telling him that he is foolish to feel that way. Or she may respond in a healthy way by saying to him, "I'm sorry to hear that. I had no idea that you were feeling that. Tell me about it." Thus she gives him a chance to share more freely what he feels, and she is able to share openly with him how she feels. If she follows the healthy approach, the couple will feel closer after the conversation. If she responds negatively, their conversation will likely revert to level 2 or level 3.

In order to stimulate communication, we must come to accept the fact that we will feel differently, even about the same thing. One may be encouraged by a sermon while another feels condemned. We must give one another the freedom to feel differently and listen sympathetically as the other shares his/her feelings. If we can develop this climate of acceptance, we will spend more and more time on this higher level of communication and our intimacy will increase.

Level 5: Loving, Genuine Truth Talk—"Let's be honest."

On this level, we are at the apex of communication. I like to picture this level as a platform upon which we can build a healthy marriage with a high degree of intimacy. This level allows us to speak the truth in love. It is where we are honest but not condemning, open but not demanding. It allows each of us the freedom to think differently and feel differently. Rather than condemning one another, we seek to understand our spouse's thoughts and feelings, looking for ways to grow together in spite of our differences.

If this sounds easy, let me assure you that it is not. If it sounds impossible, let me again assure you that it is not. It is true that many couples experience little communication on this level, but a growing number of couples are finding that with the help of God this kind of open loving communication leads to a deep sense of oneness and intimacy in their marriage. What is required is an attitude of acceptance. We want to create an atmosphere in which both of us feel safe—safe to share thoughts and feelings honestly and to know that our spouse will seek to understand, even if they do not agree with us. We come to genuinely believe that our spouse desires our best interest. If we request help, they will seek to help but will not force us to agree with their thoughts and feelings.

Some couples may ask, "Is it desirable to share with each other all of our thoughts and all of our feelings?" The answer is no. Some years ago in secular psychology, there was an emphasis on openness and honesty, where couples were encouraged to share every thought and feeling with the idea that they would have more intimacy. That school of thought was short-lived. Many marriages were devastated by such a philosophy.

The fact is that all of us have wild, crazy thoughts and feelings from time to time. Is there a husband who has never thought of running off and losing himself in a crowd? Is there a wife who has never had similar thoughts? Some thoughts are so wild and crazy or so negative that they don't deserve the dignity of being shared. I remember several years ago counseling a young couple during this emphasis on complete honesty in which the husband had come home three months after marriage and shared with his wife, "I was down at the restaurant today and saw a waitress whom I had met in college, and to be honest with you, I had the desire to date her." The wife was devastated that her husband could think of such a thing after only three months of marriage. She concluded that he could not possibly have such feelings and still love her. All of his insistence that it was a momentary thought and that the waitress meant nothing to him could not allay his wife's fears, and in fact, some months later, the couple separated.

Such thoughts should be shared with God alone. In 2 Corinthians 10:5 Paul said that we are to take "every thought captive to the obedience of Christ." The Christian's answer to such thoughts and feelings is to share them with God and to move on to face life positively with God's guidance. To share such thoughts and feelings with one's spouse is often devastating. On the other hand, to privately foster such thoughts and desires will also be devastating to the marriage. It is far better to follow the biblical pattern of bringing such thoughts and feelings to God, submitting them to his authority, turning from them when they are evil, and thanking God that we do not have to be controlled by such thoughts and feelings.

❧ ❧ ❧

Developing an awareness of these five levels of communication opens the potential for helping us enhance the quality of our communication. As you continue reading this book, I hope that you will climb the stairs together and spend more time on the platform of loving, genuine, truth talk. It may not be a steady progression. You may take two steps forward and one step back. But as you talk more, you will have a taste of communication on all five levels and recognize that all are important. As you spend more time on the higher levels, you will experience greater intimacy. The remainder of this book is devoted to helping you build the skills that lead to more effective communication and deeper intimacy.

In the next two chapters we will focus on self-understanding. You must know yourself before you can share yourself with your spouse.

CHAPTER EIGHT

GETTING
TO KNOW YOURSELF:
EXPERIENCES AND
WHAT THEY MEAN

An amazing feature of our humanity is our individual unique-ness. We have unique fingerprints, footprints, lip prints, and even voice prints. We are also unique in the way we interpret life. Suppose two people are standing on the south rim of the Grand Canyon. One stands in awe, drinking in the beauty of the shapes and colors while the other says, "I can't believe you brought me up here to see a hole in the ground." Just as each snowflake is different from all others, each individual differs in hundreds of ways from all other individuals in spite of the fact that we may live in the same culture, speak the same language, and have many common experiences.

How well do you know the unique person who lives in your body? The Scriptures indicate that God knows you inti-mately. The psalmist said to God, "For it was You who created my inward parts; You knit me together in my mother's womb. I will praise You because I am unique in remarkable ways. Your works are wonderful, and I know [this] very well" (Ps. 139:13–14). You were made by God and made in his "image." Therefore, as Ethel Waters, the beloved gospel singer, often said "God don't make no junk." Whatever your past, whatever you may have been told by others, the truth is that you are supremely valuable.

The Scriptures also teach that as a Christian you are uniquely gifted by God and that God has placed you in his body to perform a vital function (see 1 Cor. 12:12–27). As a member of his body, you alone can fulfill the role in which he has placed you. No one can make your unique contribution. The Scriptures also teach that "even the hairs of your head have all been counted" (Matt. 10:30) and that God knows everything about you (see Ps. 139:1–3; Jer. 1:4–5). If God has taken the time to know you so thoroughly and if you are such a valuable person to him, don't you think that perhaps you should spend some time getting better acquainted with yourself?

Some people are reluctant to study self-awareness, fearing that they might not like what they discover. Even though we are made in the "image" of God, we are also fallen creatures. Thus, there is always the possibility that we will discover things about ourselves with which we are not pleased. The good news is that all of the important things in our lives are changeable and, therefore, correctable. In fact, such change is the central theme of the Bible. God is active in making it possible for his children to reach the potential for which he created them. With that in mind, we should be willing to run the risk of developing deeper self-awareness.

In this chapter and the next we are going to look at five aspects of developing self-understanding: examining our experiences, interpretations, emotions, desires, and behaviors. These five aspects are constantly interacting with one another. Although we are going to examine them one by one, they do not appear or operate in sequential order. Ultimately, they cannot be separated. The combination of these aspects working together at any given point in time reveals who we are at the moment.

We Experience Life through the Five Senses

What would life be like if we did not have our five senses, if you could see nothing, hear nothing, taste nothing, smell nothing, and had no awareness of touching anything? To be sure, life is more than what we experience through our five senses, but it is difficult even to imagine life without taste, smell, touch, sight, and hearing. Even our knowledge of and experience with God has largely come to us through the five senses. We have read God's revelation in Scripture, we have heard of God's mighty acts in history, our emotions are stirred in worship when we hear the great hymns of the church. It is by means of our senses that we experience most of life. The soul of man is not dependent upon the five senses, but it is fed through them.

Throughout our waking hours we are constantly seeing, hearing, tasting, feeling, and smelling our world. Most of us take it all for granted and give little thought to the process of sensory experience—until, of course, we lose one of our senses or it becomes diminished, such as loss of hearing or loss of sight. Then we become keenly aware of what we took for granted.

The value of becoming more aware of what we are receiving through our senses is that we tend to appreciate more deeply this God-given ability. Anyone can develop their sense of self-awareness by concentrating on what they are receiving through their five senses. For example, as you read this material, focus on each of the five senses and ask yourself, "What am I seeing right now?" as you look around and observe all of the phenomena within your spectrum of sight at the moment. Pause a moment and listen to the sounds that are all around you, or see what you can touch with your hand where you are sitting. A few of you are probably snacking while you are reading this material. What do you taste? Is it sour, sweet, salty, bitter? When you concentrate on the sense of smell, what aroma floats in the air? It doesn't take much concentration to greatly enhance your awareness of the world around you.

My son and I once visited Rocky Mountain National Park, north of Denver, Colorado. Walking on the tundra trail, I *saw* some mountain formations I had never seen. I *touched* the snow that remained in the July sun. I stooped to *smell* the brilliant flowers that snuggled against the tundra surface, and I *heard* the wind grumble as it was parted by the rocks. I had a sensory experience.

Sitting at my desk writing these lines, I am far removed from that experience, but it is part of me, and I have shared that bit of me with you. Life is filled with such experiences. In fact, these experiences are the raw material from which life is made. The more we are in touch with our senses, the more we experience life.

We can train ourselves to become more attentive to our senses and thus to experience more of life. An individual who has lost sensory abilities, such as a blind person, will likely compensate by being more attentive to the other senses. For example, many blind persons have a much more highly developed sense of touch than do seeing persons.

Does being a Christian have any impact upon your sensory experience? Your immediate response may be no. Although Christians and non-Christians experience the world in much the same way through the five senses, what we choose to see, hear, touch, taste, and smell may be affected by our belief system. For example, the non-Christian may never have tasted the unleavened wafer normally served at the Lord's Supper. Hopefully, the Christian will never experience how the world looks through intoxicated eyes. There may also be certain sights and sounds to which the Christian does not wish to expose himself. In a similar manner, the non-Christian may choose never to hear Christian music. Thus, even on the sensory level our experiences are affected by our Christian beliefs.

Experience Leads to Interpretation

What we experience through the five senses, we interpret. We are thinkers; we attach meaning to what we have experienced. Our interpretations of life's experiences are influenced by our past experience, our present frame of mind, and our visions of the future. This explains why you and your spouse can observe the same phenomenon and interpret it differently. For example, you both observe a female single adult who visits your marrieds' Sunday school class. One of you interprets, "She is here to steal someone's husband." The other interprets, "It's great that she feels secure enough about herself to fellowship with married couples and not feel out of place."

Individuals almost always interpret experiences somewhat differently. Two men notice a woman smiling at them. One interprets, "She likes me." The other interprets, "She is laughing at me; she thinks I look odd." Who knows which is correct? Only the woman who smiled knows. Perhaps neither man is correct, but each will likely behave according to his own interpretation.

Our interpretations of life's experiences greatly influence both our emotions and our behavior. For example, suppose you are away from home all day Saturday. You return late Saturday night, walk into the kitchen, and find the sink filled with dirty dishes. There is a note on the table that reads, "Darling, I am attending a program at the church. May be late. Love you." The note is signed by your spouse. You have had a sensory experience: dishes in the sink, note from your spouse. Now you make an interpretation of that experience. Perhaps that interpretation will be, "He/she expects me to wash the dishes." Based upon this interpretation, you may feel upset, angry, or even resentful, and you may decide not to wash the dishes. On the other hand, you may interpret your sensory experience in a different way: "He/she must have been in a hurry; probably had some unexpected things turn up." Based upon this interpretation, you may feel sympathy, concern, or even love for your spouse, so you decide to wash the dishes. Obviously, your feelings and behavior were greatly affected by your interpretation of the sensory experience.

As noted earlier, our interpretations of life are influenced by our past experiences, our present frame of mind, and our vision of the future. This is easy to observe in the above illustration. If your past experience has been that your spouse often leaves dishes in the sink expecting you to wash them, then you are likely to conclude that this is, in fact, the case in the present experience. If, however, he/she is the kind of person who almost always washes the dishes immediately after the meal and seldom leaves the dishes in the sink, you are more likely to conclude that there had to be some extenuating circumstances for them to leave the dishes on this occasion.

It is easy also to see how your present frame of mind would influence your interpretation. If you have had a super day—all of your goals and objectives have been accomplished, everything has fallen into place, and you are feeling like a million dollars—then you may be more inclined to interpret the dirty dishes as a sign of time pressure, and you therefore tackle the task of washing them with the enthusiasm of a hungry man eating a bowl of soup. If, on the other hand, you had a difficult day—things have not fallen into place, you have accomplished none of the goals you set out to accomplish, and you feel that your day has been a total waste of time—then you may be more inclined to think that your spouse is shirking his/her responsibilities, so you avoid the dishes like the plague.

Your "vision of the future" may also affect your interpretation. If you have visions of a cozy, romantic evening, you may be more inclined to interpret the dirty dishes as an indication of your spouse's time pressure. On the other hand, if you have your mind on a TV movie that you have been anticipating watching all day, then you may be more inclined to see the dirty dishes as a sign of your spouse's laziness.

In the situation described above, you do not know the motivation of your spouse, and you have only limited knowledge of the situation. All you have is your present sensory experience: you see the dishes and you read the note. The only way to know his/her true motivation for certain is to get honest feedback from your spouse as to what he/she was thinking, feeling, and expecting when they left the dishes in the sink. If you do not check out your interpretation, then in your mind your interpretation becomes fact, and you feel and behave accordingly. This is a major factor in misunderstandings between spouses. We assume that our interpretation is fact, and often we fail to clarify our interpretation with those who may be able to give us additional information. All interpretations should be held in a tentative way, and we should always be willing to change our interpretation if we gather new information on the situation.

As humans, we seem compelled to make sense of things. Whatever we see, hear, feel, taste, or smell, we interpret; we draw conclusions; we form opinions or ideas or beliefs about those things. Two persons look at a red rose. One interprets, "Isn't God amazing? Look at the lines in that flower," while another interprets, "I wonder what the horticulturist did to produce a rose like this?" The interpretation is obviously influenced by the individual's belief system. The importance of this aspect of self-awareness is noted in Proverbs 23:7: "As he thinks within himself, so he is." Thus, a large part of understanding myself is being aware of the interpretations I give to the experiences of life. Distinguishing between the event and the interpretation is extremely important.

Your spouse isn't home at the usual time. How you interpret the event will affect your emotions and behavior. Something that looks like lipstick is on your husband's collar. How you interpret what you see will affect your emotions and behavior. Thus, it is extremely important to collect as much information as possible before making your final interpretation.

∾ ∾ ∾

Experiences and how we interpret them are two aspects of understanding who we are. In chapter 9, we look at three other elements of self-understanding.

GETTING TO KNOW YOURSELF: EMOTIONS, DESIRES, AND CHOICES

We are not computers. We have emotional responses to the situations in which we find ourselves. Feelings are spontaneous emotions that arise in response to what we experience. When I see lightning flash through the sky, I may feel afraid. When you put your arm around me, I may feel secure or loved. When you make a negative comment about the way I have painted the wall, I may feel discouraged. When you tell me that we are going on vacation next month, I may feel great happiness. When you walk across the freshly shampooed carpet with muddy shoes, I may feel upset, angry, or frustrated.

Emotions Are Uniquely Personal

Perhaps the most unique thing about us is our emotions. Rarely will two people feel the same about a given sensory experience. Even if we use the same word to describe our feelings, such as "I feel disappointed that we did not get to go to the program," we will differ in the level of disappointment. Only you know what you are feeling and how deeply you feel it. Often we are influenced by our feelings without being consciously aware of what we are feeling. Self-awareness in the area of emotions will give us greater self-understanding.

We have commonly divided emotions into two categories: positive and negative. In the positive category we list such emotions as happy, excited, thrilled, and satisfied. In the negative column we list such feelings as anger, fear, resentment, and depression. Normally, the positive emotions are those feelings that draw us toward a person, place, or thing; while negative emotions are those feelings that push us away from a person, place, or thing. For example, if I feel loved by you, then I am drawn to be with you; if I feel resentment toward you, however, then I will likely withdraw physically and emotionally.

As Christians, it is important to understand that negative emotions are not sinful. Feelings, both negative and positive, are not right or wrong; they simply are. You are human and therefore you feel. Some will read Colossians 3:8, "Put away . . . anger," and conclude that anger must be sinful. However, Paul's warning was addressed to the issue of allowing anger to live inside over a long period of time. We are told in Ephesians 4:26 that we are not to let the sun go down on our anger. We are not told that anger is sinful. Anger is meant to be a temporary visitor indicating to us that something needs our attention. But anger is never to be a resident in our hearts. Jesus felt anger on more than one occasion (Mark 3:5; 10:14). Christians are sometimes shocked to discover that Jesus also had feelings of discouragement and even depression (Matt. 26:37–38). Although Jesus was divine, he was also fully human, and his emotions ran the gamut of both positive and negative feelings.

Therefore, you do not have to apologize for your emotions. Your emotions, however, do tell you something about yourself. They give you some clues as to how you are responding to the present situation. They are like the indicator lights on the instrument panel of your car, informing you that something needs your attention. You can ignore the little red engine light, or you can get out and put in a quart of oil. The same is true with your emotions. You can ignore a negative emotion, or you can give your attention to doing something constructive in the area to which the emotion is related. You cannot get rid of feelings by trying to deny them, nor can you control them by ignoring them. If you ignore the red engine light, it is only a matter of time until you will be stopped by the malfunctioning of your car. If you ignore your negative emotions, you will be stopped just as surely by the malfunctioning of your body and your relationships.

You can change emotions by reexamining your interpretation of the situation or by getting more information. Let's say that you are standing in front of the dirty dishes situation described in chapter 8 when your teenage son arrives. He informs you that your spouse spent the afternoon in the emergency room with your youngest daughter, who cut her finger and required several stitches. Immediately upon receiving this information, your emotions will likely change toward your spouse. Usually we do not get additional information unless we ask for it. But as you can see, it is well worth seeking.

Notice four things about emotions. *First,* they normally appear spontaneously. We don't sit around thinking, *I believe now I will go out and feel lonely.* Loneliness is a feeling that overtakes us, not something we choose to feel.

Second, emotions often come in groups. That is, many times we feel more than one emotion. If you are involved in an automobile accident, immediately you may feel angry, frustrated, irritated, anxious, and cautious, all at the same time.

Third, emotions have different levels of intensity. You may feel mildly happy or exceedingly happy. You may feel somewhat sad, or you may be in the pits.

Finally, your feelings may sometimes be in conflict with one another. Your spouse tells you that he has just made a $500 purchase—a real bargain, for the item normally sells for $998. You may feel happy that he has made such a savings and, at the same time, fearful that you do not have enough money to cover the purchase since you made a $300 purchase you have not told him about.

Your teenager son comes home an hour after you expected him. You may feel relieved that he is home and happy that he is safe. But you may also feel angry that he was not thoughtful enough to call.

Being in touch with your emotions will give you a better understanding of who you are and why you behave the way you do. One way to enhance your awareness of your emotions is to simply ask the question, "What am I feeling right now?" Another way to enhance your sensitivity to your feelings is to observe the way you are physically responding. Are you smiling as you hear the person talk? Do you have eye contact with her? What is the tone of your voice? Your physical responses to a situation often give you a clue to what you are feeling. Your feelings at any given moment reveal one aspect of who you are. When you say, "I feel angry right now" or "I feel happy today," you are describing something of who you are. Feelings are an important part of our lives, and they greatly influence our behavior.

Desires Reveal the Heart

We are creatures of desire. That is, we want certain things, or we want to be a certain way, or we want other people to do certain things. Desires are usually expressed in terms of "I want . . . ," "I wish . . . ," "I hope . . . ," or "I would like. . . ." These desires may be long-range ("I hope someday to be a millionaire") or short-term ("I would like to take Tuesday afternoon off and play golf"). In all areas of life, we are filled with desires. We desire certain material things, and we desire certain things in our marriage relationship. These desires often set the stage for our actions. For example, "I want my wife to feel loved" may be impetus for buying her a dozen roses.

As you read this chapter, you may not be consciously thinking of any desires, but with a moment's reflection, you can probably list numerous ones. In terms of the material world, you may desire a new gas grill, new window treatments for the family room, carpet for the bedroom, new car, or new clothes. In the spiritual realm, you may desire to become more effective in sharing your faith, more consistent in your daily quiet time with God, more forgiving in your attitude toward others, or more liberal in your giving. In your relationship with your spouse, you may desire more communication, less arguing, more affection, or a higher level of sexual satisfaction. On and on the list could go—in every area of life, we have desires.

Not all desires are of the same value. In fact, some of our desires may actually be evil or selfish desires. We are warned in Scripture to turn away from such desires. Paul indicated that the failures of ancient Israel should be an example to us "so that we will not desire evil as they did" (1 Cor. 10:6). Jesus made it clear that to foster such desires is sinful. "But I tell you, everyone who looks at a woman to lust for her has already committed adultery with her in his heart" (Matt. 5:28).

We cannot keep evil desires from entering the mind, but we do not have to feed them. Martin Luther is attributed with saying, "We cannot keep the birds from flying over our heads, but we do not have to let them build nests in our hair." Paul instructed us to be "taking every thought captive to the obedience of Christ" (2 Cor. 10:5). The word that is translated *captive* means literally "to put a net around." It is the picture of catching a butterfly in a net. We are to take our desires captive or put nets around them and bring them to God and place them under his lordship. If they are in fact evil desires, they are to be committed to him and not pursued. If they are wholesome desires, then we are to apply our energies to bringing them to pass.

Being aware of our desires is the first step to being able to judge whether they are good or bad, loving or selfish. Remember, it is not sinful to have an evil or selfish desire; it is sinful to feed that desire and to act upon it. Some Christians feel guilty when an evil desire crosses their mind. They reason that if they were really good Christians, they would not have such desires. The fact is, we are all sinners by nature, and sinful thoughts are a part of our fallen nature. The good news is that with the help of God's Spirit, we need not follow these evil desires.

I suggest the following prayer when you have an evil desire: "Lord, you know what I am thinking at the moment, but I thank you that with your power I do not have to follow that desire. Now guide me as I do something constructive with my life." Then move out to take some constructive action. Such a prayer does not always remove the evil desire from your mind, but it does channel your energies into positive and constructive activity. You have brought the desire to God and have put it under the lordship of Christ.

As with our feelings, our desires may be in conflict. "I want to go with my spouse to the symphony, but I also want to be at the church softball tournament." Desires may also vary in intensity. I may rank my desire to be a millionaire at 5 on a scale of 0 to 10, while I rank my desire to spend time with my children at 10.

Desires often motivate us to action. This is extremely positive when our desires are wholesome. Becoming aware of our desires and evaluating their value is an important part of self-awareness. One of the ways to foster conscious awareness of our desires is to think of several areas of life and complete the following sentence: "One of the things I desire in this area of life is . . . ." You may include the following areas: "One of the things I desire in my spiritual life is . . . ." "One of the things I desire vocationally is . . . ." "One of the things I desire for my children is . . . ." "One of the things I desire for my marriage is . . . ." The desires were in your heart before you completed those sentences; the exercise simply helped reveal them.

Behavior Reveals the Reality of Choice

A "don't just stand there; do something" mentality seems to be a part of our humanity. We are creatures of action. In response to our sensory experience and our interpretation of that experience with our feelings and desires, we decide to behave in certain ways. At the moment, our decision seems logical; it all makes sense, most of the time. Our behavior is the most observable part of our lives. It is that part of us from which others draw their opinions. Jesus said, "You'll recognize them by their fruit" (Matt. 7:16). On another occasion Jesus said, "All people will know that you are My disciples, if you have love for one another" (John 13:35).

It is obvious that Jesus' reference to love implied observable acts that demonstrated inner concern. The actions are observed by others, not the inner concern. Thus, our behavior is extremely important in our ministry to others.

Normally, when our behavior is positive and appropriate, we feel good about our choices. When our behavior is sinful, we feel ashamed or guilty. If I have wronged my spouse, I feel guilty. Since I desire to be in fellowship with God and my spouse, I am motivated to say, "I am sorry. I was wrong. Will you forgive me?" My spouse hears my confession, sees my facial expression, interprets my sincerity, and feels sympathy for me. Having a desire to do what is right and to be Christlike, she chooses to forgive me, and the relationship is restored.

Sometimes we become aware of our behavior only when others point it out to us. Often while I am driving down the road, my wife reaches over and pats me on the arm. I know immediately that I am exceeding the speed limit. Before the pat on the arm, I am totally unaware of my behavior. Your husband may say to you, "I like the way you smile when you sing in the choir." Before his comment, you may have been unaware of your smiling while singing. Becoming aware of your behavior will help you understand your spouse's response to you. I have often encountered couples in counseling who were unaware of their negative speech patterns to each other and how these affected their spouse's response. After we become aware of behavior patterns, we have the possibility of changing them if we so choose.

There is both a spiritual dimension and a human dimension to changing our behavior. The spiritual dimension is what Paul referred to in his own life when he said, "I do not understand what I am doing, because I do not practice what I want to do, but I do what I hate.... For the desire to do what is good is with me, but there is no ability to do it. For I do not do the good that I want to do, but I practice the evil that I do not want to do. Now if I do what I do not want, I am no longer the one doing it, but it is the sin that lives in me" (Rom. 7:15, 18–20).

After discussing this spiritual struggle, Paul indicates that it is through the power of the Holy Spirit in our lives that we are set free from the bondage of the sinful nature and are enabled to accomplish the good that we desire (Rom. 8:1–2). Thus, as Christians, we know that the ultimate power for right living is in yielding ourselves to the Holy Spirit and allowing him to control our behavior.

But there is a human dimension to our behavior, and that is the focus of this chapter. Behind human behavior is always our sensory experience, our interpretation of that experience, our feelings, and our desires. If we want an understanding of why we do the things we do, it will be found in becoming more aware of these four aspects of ourselves. In the course of living life daily, most of this is carried on at the subconscious level. That is, we are not consciously aware of what we are feeling, what our desires are, and how we are interpreting our sensory experience. But when we are willing to give attention to these matters and develop more self-awareness, we will not only understand our behavior better, we are far more likely to end up behaving in a constructive and positive manner.

Notice that the five aspects of self-awareness we have discussed— experience, interpretation, emotions, desires, and behavior—are all interrelated. One logically leads to another, but at times we may focus more on one than the other. Often we are more in touch with one aspect of ourselves than we are with another. For example, in the earlier example of the two individuals looking into the Grand Canyon, one has his *feelings* in focus—he drinks in the beauty, the colors, the depth, and the magnitude of the canyon. The other is more in tune with his *desires*— perhaps for a juicy hamburger or a cold drink—thus, he sees the canyon simply as a big hole in the ground from which he is ready to withdraw to something more exciting. To be fully aware of who we are at the moment is to be in touch with all five aspects of self-awareness.

In Western society there has been a tendency to exalt emotions and desires at the expense of reason and choice. We hear a great deal of talk about "being true to oneself." A husband says, "I've got to be true to myself. I just don't love her anymore." He uses this as an excuse for leaving his wife. Or a wife says, "I must be honest with myself. I hate my husband, and I don't want to live with him anymore," so she splits.

Notice carefully that in both of these statements, reference is made to *feelings*. The husband uses the word *love*—"I don't love her." The wife uses the word *hate*. Both of these are emotions. In these two statements, the individuals are concluding that their feelings are most important. Therefore, they are basing their behavior on their feelings.

This is a common error. In our society we have tended to exalt our *feelings* and our *desires* as being most important. That is, we have concluded that what I feel and what I desire is the real me. This is a serious mistake, and it is not in keeping with what the Bible teaches. From the wisdom literature of the Bible we read, "For as he *thinketh* in his heart, so is he" (Prov. 23:7 KJV, italics added). The emphasis here is on *thoughts* not feelings. In the New Testament we read: "Finally, brothers, whatever is true, whatever is noble, whatever is right, whatever is pure, whatever is lovely, whatever is admirable—if anything is excellent or praiseworthy— *think* about such things. Whatever you have learned or received or heard from me or seen in me—*put it into practice*. And the God of peace will be with you" (Phil. 4:8–9 NIV, italics added). Note the emphasis in these verses on *thinking* and *behaving*. The way we interpret life's experiences and the way we respond to them are far more important than how we feel or what we desire.

Let me illustrate from the life of our Lord. Jesus was near the end of his life, only hours away from the cross: "Then Jesus went with his disciples to a place called Gethsemane, and he said to them, 'Sit here while I go over there and pray.' He took Peter and the two sons of Zebedee along with him, and he began to be *sorrowful and troubled*. Then he said to them, 'My soul is *overwhelmed with sorrow* to the point of death. Stay here and keep watch with me.' Going a little farther, he fell with his face to the ground and prayed. 'My Father, if it is possible, may this cup be taken from me. Yet not as I will, but as you will'" (Matt. 26:36–39 NIV, italics added).

Notice carefully the italicized words. What were the feelings of Jesus? He was sorrowful and troubled, overwhelmed with sorrow. What were his desires? "If it be possible, may this cup be taken from me?" But how does he interpret the situation. "Yet not as I will, but as you will." The will of the Father was more important than Jesus' present feelings or desires. His subsequent behavior was based not on his feelings or on his momentary desire for relief from the cup of pain but on his interpretation that life is not to be controlled by feelings and desires but by the will of God.

This is an important lesson for us to learn, especially in a society that has exalted emotions and desires and made us think that if we do not follow our feelings and desires, we will never be happy. The fact is that our feelings and desires must always be integrated with the intellect and will. It is the worst form of immaturity to allow one's feelings and desires to control life. Our mind judges the wisdom of acting upon certain emotions, and our will carries out our decision. For example, I may fear telling the truth to my spouse about having forgotten to pick up the laundry at the dry cleaners. My mind decides that I should not act on this fear. My will carries out the decision to tell the truth. If we are going to exalt any two of the five factors of self-awareness, it should be the interpretation of our sensory experiences and our behavior. These are of utmost importance.

Does this mean that desires and feelings are therefore unimportant? By no means. They are a vital part of our personhood and cannot be ignored or denied. It is only as we are in touch with our emotions and our desires that we are able to analyze them and make wise decisions about our behavior. The way we think, however, greatly influences the way we feel. I have the choice in any situation to think the best of my spouse or to think the worst. If I think the worst, then almost inevitably I will have feelings of anger and resentment. If I think the best, at least my feelings will be neutral for the moment, maybe even positive. If I choose to think the best, I may be disappointed when more information reveals that I was wrong, but at least I will be in a better frame of mind to process the negative reality.

As Christians, we have tremendous help in building our marriages. Not only do we have the ability to develop self-awareness, as do non-Christians, but we have the added insight of Scripture and the aid of the Holy Spirit to interpret life and to guide our thoughts and behavior. The couple who will use these resources will be light-years ahead of non-Christians in building a happy marriage.

Let me illustrate by using the husband who no longer loves his wife and feels that he must leave her. A Christian who has such feelings and desires would also likely feel frustrated because he knows Scripture teaches that he is to love his wife as Christ loved the church (Eph. 5:25). He also knows that the Bible teaches that marriage is forever and that God hates divorce (Mal. 2:16). So what is the husband to do? Hopefully, he will take his struggle to God and ask for wisdom. He will begin to search the Scriptures to find direction. One of the principles of the Bible is that in the multitude of counselors, there is safety (Prov. 11:14). Thus, in obedience to Scripture, the husband may go for counseling or he may begin to read a Christian book to see how others have handled similar feelings and desires. In taking either of these actions, he will likely discover that what he is feeling and desiring is rather common; that the intensity of the euphoric, romantic feelings in a marriage relationship come and go in the ebb and flow of life; and that there may be periods in which we almost lose such feelings. There are reasons for this, and those reasons normally relate to unmet emotional or physical needs. He will also learn that there are ways to revive those positive, romantic feelings in his relationship.

Hopefully he will come to a place where he can lovingly share his struggle with his wife. Ideally she will allow her commitment to Christ to motivate her to take a fresh look at the foundations of her marriage, be open to new understandings, and work with him to rebuild a loving relationship. In time they may each come to experience the rebirth of romantic feelings and have a much deeper, more meaningful relationship. Thus, the husband's willingness to allow his Christian interpretation of life to influence his behavior more fully than his feelings and desires will reap the fruit of such wisdom. On the other hand, his non-Christian friend, who has no knowledge of such resources, will likely continue to follow his emotions and desires and will experience the results of such folly. If we get in touch with all five factors of self-awareness, we are more likely to make responsible decisions.

ક્ર ક્ર ક્ર

When we have greater self-awareness, we are more fully prepared to share our lives with our spouses. In chapter 10 we will examine the process of self-revelation, which enhances intimacy.

CHAPTER TEN

LEARNING THE ART OF SELF-REVELATION

You may be asking, "What is the big deal about self-awareness. I know I experience life through the five senses. I know I attach meaning to what I experience. I know that I have emotions and desires, and I know that I make choices—so why spend so much time on getting in touch with myself?" The big deal is not self-awareness; the big deal is *marital intimacy*. Covenant marriage, as described in the Bible, is not two people living in the same house. Rather, it is two people whose hearts and lives are bonded together in deep intimacy. Such intimacy, however, requires revealing to each other the inner self. Self-awareness is a prerequisite to such sharing. How can I tell you who I am if I don't know who I am?

Self-awareness and self-disclosure are the processes whereby a couple builds marital intimacy. In the act of self-revelation, I often gain a clearer perspective on how I really feel or what my true desires are. A wife says, "I feel disappointed that you didn't introduce me to your friend. Well, it's not so much that you didn't introduce me; it's that I felt I was not important to you. If I had been important, I think you would have introduced me." This wife is gaining fuller self-awareness as she seeks to reveal her feelings to her husband. Our purpose in self-revelation is to be known by our spouse, to gain closeness and intimacy in our relationship, to be understood, and to allow our uniqueness to be known to each other.

The most fundamental principle of self-revelation is learning to speak for yourself. This is often explained by communication experts as using "I" statements rather than "you" statements. If I start my sentence with "I" and then attempt to reveal not only what I have experienced but also my emotions, desires, and behavior, perhaps you will know me better. The following discourse contains examples of common "I" statements: "I heard you say that you were planning to play golf on Saturday. I understand that to mean that you will not be able to go with me to my mother's birthday party. I feel disappointed by that. I had hoped that we could both be there. I am sharing this because I realize that I may have misunderstood what you said, or perhaps you have forgotten about mother's birthday party. I would like to know your thoughts and feelings. I don't want this to be a barrier between us."

On the other hand, "you" statements attempt to do what is ultimately impossible: speak for your spouse. It implies that you have read their mind and know their thoughts, feelings, and desires. The same discourse with "you" statements would sound like the following: "You said you were going to play golf this Saturday. You know that is the day of my mother's birthday party. You don't ever think about me and my feelings. You only think about Number One and what you want to do." Such "you" statements assume that you know your spouse's intentions, thoughts, and desires.

Not all "you" statements are condemning. A wife may say to a husband, "You love me. You know you love me. You've always been so kind to me. You always want to do what would make me happy. You are so thoughtful and kind." Such "you" statements may be simply setting the husband up to be manipulated to do what the wife desires.

When I make such statements as "You are angry," "You don't really appreciate me," "You should be working on the car instead of watching television," I dogmatically say things that are actually only my perceptions. Such communication usually produces resentment in the other person because I am speaking beyond my knowledge and, in some cases, I am speaking as though I were God and know what the other person ought to be doing.

"I" statements, on the other hand, honestly report our own experience—what we are sensing, thinking, feeling, desiring, and doing. "I feel tired," "I think you made a good point," and "I wish we could go shopping tonight" reveal something of who you are at the moment. "I" statements are always better than "you" statements when trying to communicate to your spouse.

Another pitfall in communication is to use "they" statements. Such statements tend to be general and speak for a larger body. For example: "They say that in a good marriage each person should have some spending money." "Some people think it is wrong for mothers-in-law to live with couples." "Most people would think that two hours would be long enough to buy a child a pair of shoes." "They say that women are more emotional than men." In these statements, the speaker is clearly not taking responsibility for the content. It is not clear whether he or she agrees with the statement although it is assumed that he or she probably does. It is far better to speak for yourself than to quote what "they" think.

Revealing Our Experiences

We reveal our experiences when we describe something we see, hear, touch, taste, or smell. We give our spouse the benefit of our sensory experience. We expose our spouse to the raw data from which we have drawn interpretations and share our sensory experiences related to their behavior. For example, Mary may share with Bill: "I noticed Thursday night when we bought the shoes for Bobby that when you wrote the check, you were shaking your head back and forth. This led me to believe that you felt that the shoes cost too much. Was I reading you correctly?" This statement gives Bill the opportunity to either affirm her conclusion or to clarify what he had in mind by his behavior, and it lets him know the sensory experience from which she reached her conclusion.

A husband may say to his wife, "Last night when we left the Foster's, I heard you say to Mrs. Foster, 'I will see you next week.' Are you in a Bible study group or something?" The wife responds, "No, I usually see her at Robby's soccer practice. Her son Jamie is on Robby's team." "I sensed that you were a little uncomfortable when she started talking about spiritual things. Was I right or wrong?" "You were right. She's a little pushy for me. I felt like she was overly dogmatic about her beliefs. I don't think her idea of dead people becoming angels is a biblical idea." Note that in each of these statements, the couple uses "I" statements. They are sharing how they feel and think. The conversation will likely proceed in a positive way as long as each of them continues to speak for themselves and not for each other or for Mrs. Foster.

Usually when we share what we have heard, seen, smelled, tasted, or touched, we give *our* interpretation of our experience. For example, Art said to Jenna, "When I walked out of the house this morning, I noticed that you looked at me and smiled. I take that to mean that you have forgiven me for getting home late last night?" By giving Jenna the observation he made about her behavior (a smile), he gave her some idea of how he reached his conclusion that perhaps she had forgiven him. Jenna then has the opportunity to affirm or deny her forgiveness.

Your spouse is much more likely to understand your conclusion if he/she understands the sensory experience upon which you based it. They may or may not agree with your conclusion, but at least they know the logic behind it.

Perhaps the best way to share your experiences is to focus on the five senses—hearing, seeing, smelling, tasting, and touching. Practice completing the following sentences and you will be developing the art of self-revelation: "I think I heard you say . . . ." "When I came in tonight, I think I saw you . . . ." "When I walked into the house and smelled . . . ." "When I tasted your vegetable soup . . . ." "When I hugged you this afternoon . . . ." Begin by sharing what you saw, heard, smelled, tasted, or touched; then share your conclusions or interpretations.

Revealing Your Interpretations

Some couples are not accustomed to sharing their interpretations of sensory experience. They simply draw conclusions and act accordingly. This accounts for much misunderstanding in marriage relationships. My spouse may have no idea why I am responding the way I am because she does not realize the conclusions I have drawn from what I have observed.

Interpretations are based on our limited experience; thus, we should always hold our conclusion as temporary until we have shared them with our spouse. Additional information may shed new light on our conclusion. For example, Brenda says to Rod, "When I was talking with you earlier tonight, I noticed that you fell asleep. I felt like you were not interested in what I was saying. Is that true?" Rod responds, "No, dear, I am interested in what you are saying. It's just that last night I didn't sleep very well, and I've been extremely tired today." We should never assume our conclusion is accurate but should always give our spouses opportunity to clarify. What is important is that we reveal to our spouse what we are thinking.

If Brenda had not verbally shared with Rod her interpretation of his behavior, the outcome would have been totally different. She may have observed his behavior (falling asleep while she was talking), made her conclusion (he's not interested in what I am saying), and simply withdrawn and stopped talking for the rest of the evening. In fact, she may have been cold toward him for several hours or even days. He would have observed her behavior without explanation as to why. Thus, he would have drawn his own conclusion, perhaps feeling rejected by her and, in turn, resentful toward her. He also may have withdrawn further. All of this misunderstanding and hurt feelings could have been avoided, as it was in our illustration when Brenda shared her interpretation with Rod and asked for clarification. Much of the hurt, pain, and misunderstanding in marriage can be avoided by learning to share our interpretations of our experiences and giving our spouses an opportunity to clarify.

It is important to remember to use "I" statements when sharing your interpretations. You are simply giving your spouse information about your thoughts. For example, Jan says to her husband, "I think you would enjoy the Shakespeare play. I talked with Bonnie this afternoon. She saw it last night and said . . . ." Jan is expressing her interpretation; thus, she made "I" statements. "I think you'd enjoy it," not "You would enjoy it."

Revealing Your Feelings

Most of our feelings are tied to some experience we have had in the past or the present. The next time you feel disappointed, ask, "What stimulated my disappointment?" Chances are you will find that your feeling of disappointment is tied directly to someone's behavior— perhaps your spouse's or even your own.

Suppose you had wanted to take a ride in the country after dinner. You even mentioned it to your spouse yesterday, but he/she came home two hours later than you anticipated, and a ride in the country is out of the question. If you do not share your feelings with your spouse, they will likely show up in your behavior; but your spouse may have little indication as to why you are behaving as you are. When you share your feelings and the experience upon which they are based, however, then your spouse has a clearer picture of where you are at the moment. Hopefully he/she will choose an appropriate response.

It is important here to distinguish between acting on our feelings and sharing our feelings. We certainly don't want to be controlled by our emotions. Feelings are only one aspect of determining behavior, but since we are influenced by our feelings, we will be known and understood better if we share those feelings. "I feel happy about our decision to have the tutor for Jacob." "I am discouraged with my progress on my painting." Also, remember to use "I" statements because you are only speaking for yourself: "I really enjoyed our time together at the beach," rather than "We had a good time at the beach."

Some of us were brought up not to share feelings; thus, we may find it difficult to disclose our emotions. Feelings, however, are a part of us. If we share no feelings, we cut our spouse off from a part of who we are.

Revealing Your Desires

The failure to share desires in a positive and fair manner is also the source of much misunderstanding and frustration in marriage. Expecting our spouses to fulfill our unexpressed desires is asking the impossible, and it makes disappointment inevitable. If we express our desires to our spouse, then they have the chance to seek to accommodate our desires or to refuse to be a part of seeing them fulfilled. At least, they have a chance.

I have known individuals who for years have had certain desires about how they would like to celebrate their wedding anniversary, but they have never shared these desires with their spouse. They have waited year after year, hoping that their spouse would one year surprise them. I hope they live a long time because such surprises come only about once every hundred years. How much wiser to share our desires simply and clearly so our spouse has no question about what we would like.

Letting our spouse know what we want is a vital part of self-revelation. "I want . . . ." "I wish . . . ." "Do you know what would really make me happy?" And, "I'd like . . . ." are the kinds of statements that communicate desires. Note that though these words express information and sometimes makes requests, they never make demands. For example, "I want to go to the mountains sometime this summer for a weekend" is a statement of information. Such information may be followed by a request: "Could we possibly go the third weekend in August?" You can even share both information and a request in the same statement: "When you have time, I'd like to tell you something that happened to me at work today."

Remember, it is easy to slip into speaking for the other person. For example, we speak for the other person when we say something like "You should not do that tonight because Melissa is practicing the piano." Better to say, "I wish you would not do that tonight because I think it will interfere with Melissa's piano practice." When we know each other's desires, we can then choose our actions.

We should not try to manipulate our spouse in the expression of our desires. "Don't you think it would be too crowded for us to go to the mall tonight?" is a manipulating statement. Far better to say, "I wish we would not go to the mall tonight. I think it will be too crowded." It is not our responsibility to control the decisions of our spouse. It is our responsibility to let them know what we would like.

Revealing Your Behavior

Why do I need to tell my spouse about my behavior? Can't she simply observe it? Yes and no. Though she may observe my behavior, she may not know what it means. For example, my spouse may observe that I nodded while she was talking to me, but she may not know that the headache medication I took two hours ago is making me drowsy. Yet she will understand if I say to her, "I nodded on you. I am sorry. I took headache medication a couple of hours ago, and it is making me drowsy. It's not that I don't want to hear what you have to say." She has a clearer understanding of my behavior.

Reporting on your behavior may involve past, present, and future behavior. Sharing future behavior is giving your spouse an indication of what you intend to do at some time in the future: "I plan to wash the car as soon as I get home from the ballgame." Such a statement lets your wife know what behavior she can expect from you after the game. Most spouses who receive such information find it extremely satisfying. First of all, it says that the spouse who is communicating his/her future intentions cares enough to share them. Second, it gives the spouse who receives this information an opportunity to respond. Third, it helps them to organize their own life and frees them from surprises to which they must adjust.

This morning I said to my wife, "I would like to spend the morning working in the yard, and then this afternoon, do some writing. How does that sound to you?" She thought it was great (anytime I work in the yard, it's great). She shared with me some of her plans for the day, and we both moved out to experience the day with a sense of togetherness even though we were going to spend the bulk of our time apart. The choice to inform each other of our future behavior and to allow the other's input goes a long way in building intimacy into a marriage relationship.

Sharing past behavior can also give your spouse a sense of love and concern. Let's say the two of you agree that next month you would like to begin redecorating the bedroom, including new furniture. You agree that each of you will do preliminary investigation on certain aspects of the project. Two weeks later, perhaps, both of you have been doing your homework, but if you have not shared with each other what you have done, one or both of you may be feeling that the other is not interested in the project. This misunderstanding can be avoided by sharing: "Today I went by the furniture store and checked on a bedroom suite. I really like it and I think it is a good deal. I'd like for you to look at it." Now your spouse knows that you are into the project, and he/she feels good about what you are doing.

If your spouse says, "I tried to call you before I left the office today but the line was busy; sorry I didn't get you," chances are you will take encouragement in the fact that they tried to call (unless, of course, you interpret their statement to be a condemnation for your spending too much time on the telephone). Perhaps since you are reading this chapter, you will share your interpretation and give them a chance to clarify.

Sharing present behavior may be the thing we are least inclined to do, for most of us work on the assumption that if we are with our spouses, they can see our behavior and we do not need to verbalize it. I have found, however, that spouses who learn to share present behavior, especially negative behavior, greatly improve the atmosphere for communication. "I walked out of the room while you were talking. That wasn't very thoughtful. I'm sorry. I really am trying to break that habit. I really am interested in what you are saying. Please finish your story." For some couples, such a statement would radically change their relationship.

You may say, "I'm talking too loudly. I'm sorry." You have let your spouse know that you are aware of your inappropriate speech pattern and that you are concerned about the effect of your behavior on him. Before you shared your awareness of your behavior, he was able only to observe your behavior. He did not know whether you were aware of it or how you interpreted it.

Suppose your husband walks into the room and sees you crying. He observes your behavior, but he has no idea why you are crying. When you say, "I am crying, but it has nothing to do with you. I've just been thinking about how much I miss Mom and how sad it is that I will never be able to talk with her again," you have now given your husband valuable information. He has the opportunity to give you a sympathetic hug and understanding words. He doesn't have to spend the evening wondering why you were crying and if he did something to upset you. Acknowledging your behavior and explaining what motivated it leads to understanding and intimacy.

In our conversations with each other, we would seldom share all five aspects of self-awareness in a single paragraph although we may often share two or three. For example, we may say "I am really excited about our decision to buy a microwave (feelings). I want us to get it before next weekend if possible (desires). I think it is really going to help with my time pressure (interpretation)." Another example: "As I came in I saw water running under the door from the storeroom (senses). The water heater must be leaking (interpretation). I really dread having to face that tonight (feelings), but I know it cannot wait until tomorrow, so I will check on it as soon as I wash my hands (behavior)."

Such statements help our spouse understand what we are experiencing and how we are interpreting it. It takes the guesswork out of a relationship. No longer are we trying to read each other's minds or wondering what certain behaviors mean. We are getting honest reports from each other about what we are experiencing in life and how we are interpreting it. This kind of self-awareness and self-disclosure greatly enhances a marriage relationship.

Practice self-revelation by completing the following sentences at least once a day: "I saw or heard . . . ."; "I interpreted that to mean . . . ."; "Therefore, I felt . . . ."; "I wish . . . ."; "I think I should . . . ."

With practice you will be poised to share more freely with your spouse. Learning the art of self-revelation may take effort, but the rewards are worth the work. In chapter 11 we take a look at your future growth potential.

CHAPTER ELEVEN

GETTING READY TO GROW: PRIORITIES AND GOALS

Time is passing; things are changing, but the question is, "Are we growing?" There is a vast difference between change and growth. Change tends to be random; growth tends to be directed. Growth has purpose; it moves toward an objective. If I plant a vegetable garden, the objective is not to have healthy looking plants but rather to produce tomatoes, squash, and cucumbers. Similarly in a marriage, our objective is not to live in the same house and appear to be "an ideal couple." The objective is to have an intimate relationship in which the two of us are encouraging each other to become all that God desires us to be. Getting ready to grow requires that we clarify our priorities and goals.

The Christian must make certain that his or her priorities are in keeping with God's priorities. Are my values God's values? Are the things I believe to be important in life also important to God? How closely does my view of life agree with God's view of life? If we are to be ultimately successful, we must bring our priorities in line with God's priorities.

A priority is something we believe to be important. When we list priorities, we are listing those things we believe to be of great value in life. What are the things that Christians have traditionally noted as being priorities? Most Christians would agree that priority number one is our relationship and fellowship with God. Nothing is more important. In fact, our relationship with God influences the rest of our priorities. If God is the author of life, then nothing is more important in understanding life than first knowing him (see John 17:3). If God has spoken, then nothing is more important than hearing his voice (Matt. 11:15). If he loves, nothing can bring greater joy than responding to his love (1 John 4:19). To those who seemed to be consumed with acquiring clothing, food, and shelter, Jesus said, "Your heavenly Father knows that you need them. But seek first the kingdom of God and His righteousness, and all these things will be provided for you" (Matt. 6:32–33). Notice, it is not simply having a relationship with God, but it is seeking his kingdom. It is spending time in fellowship with him to gain his perspective on life.

Another priority for most Christians is family. Believing that God established marriage and family as the most basic unit of society makes family extremely important. Within family relationships, we recognize that the marriage relationship is more fundamental than the parent–child relationship. Marriage is a lifelong, intimate relationship, whereas most children will eventually leave their parents and establish their own marriage relationships. The quality of the marriage relationship is also important because it greatly affects the parent–child relationship.

A third priority for most Christians is vocation. Some might object to listing vocation as a separate priority since a person cannot be rightly related to his or her family without making financial provision for them (1 Tim. 5:8). However, because priorities are interrelated, this criticism could be made of any list of priorities. I choose to list vocation separately because it involves such a large segment of our time. The Scriptures also emphasize the importance of vocation (Gen. 1:28; 2 Thess. 3:10). Because tension often exists between one's family life and vocation, learning to balance these two priorities requires diligence.

Most Christians would also list among their priorities their ministry through the church. Again, some would feel that our life and work in the church are not to be separated from our number one priority: our relationship with God. In the outworking of life, our ministry in the church is an outgrowth of our relationship with God (Matt. 28:18–20; Heb. 10:24–25). The church is the context in which we serve God because we know and love him. God has given each Christian spiritual gifts, and his intention is that we use these gifts to enhance the lives of other Christians and to attract non-Christians to Christ (Matt. 4:10; 1 Cor. 12:4–30; Heb. 9:14).

Believing that we are made in God's image (Gen. 1:27) and that our bodies are the temple of the Holy Spirit (1 Cor. 6:19–20), most Christians would agree that among their list of priorities would be caring for their own physical, emotional, and spiritual well-being. We are told by Jesus that we are to love our neighbor as we love ourselves (Mark 12:31). The Christian who does not give adequate attention to his own needs will not long love and serve his neighbor.

By listing these five priorities, I am not suggesting that this is a comprehensive list for Christians. Additional priorities might include such things as sports, education, civic and social clubs, political activities, and so forth. What is important is that each couple think through their priorities and be able to state them in meaningful terms. What do they view to be important in life? What are the five or ten most important things for them? We cannot reach priorities until priorities have been established.

What does a couple do when they discover that, in fact, they disagree strongly about priorities? For example, a husband may feel that his vocation is more important than time with the family. At his stage in life he perceives that more of his time, energy, and effort should be invested in "getting ahead" in his vocation. His family will have to play a secondary role until he reaches his vocational goals. This may be stated overtly, or it might be revealed as he discusses priorities. Simply observing his lifestyle may indicate that vocation seems to have priority over family.

If we, as a couple, disagree on priorities, we must first of all remember that no one can force priorities on another, not even our spouse. We cannot argue each other to "our way" of thinking. If we genuinely differ on priorities, we must acknowledge this and seek compromise so that a good measure of each of our priorities may be accomplished.

Traditionally, Christians have tended to list priorities in the following order: (1) God, (2) family, (3) vocation, (4) church, (5) personal enrichment, (6) other relationships and activities. Some Christians have squabbled over the order in which priorities are listed. A number of years ago, a friend shared with me an illustration using the human hand that I have found very helpful. The thumb represents my relationship and fellowship with God. My other priorities are listed on the four fingers. As the thumb interfaces with each of the four fingers, so my relationship with God will affect all other priorities. As I am growing in my understanding of God and in my intimacy with him, I will be more effective in reaching my priorities of family, vocation, ministry, and personal well-being. I draw from God not only wisdom but power to accomplish my other priorities.

Under the lordship of Christ, on any given day, I may spend a larger part of my time and energy on any one of the four priorities. For example, if the index finger represents "personal well-being" and today I happen to be sick, then the bulk of my time and energy may be expended on getting to the doctor and getting the medical attention I need. That does not make personal well-being more important than family or vocation. It is simply a reality that on that particular day under the guidance of the Holy Spirit, I must invest time and energy in caring for myself.

The thumb, representing God, interfaces with each of the other fingers representing other priorities. If my fellowship with God is strong, I can trust him to guide me in what should be my priority on any given day or segment of the day. If marriage and family is one of my priorities, and today happens to be our wedding anniversary, then chances are God will have me spend a significant amount of time and energy in celebrating our marriage. When we think of priorities in this way, it is obvious that fellowship with God becomes extremely important since it greatly influences our attention to other priorities in life. Taking time to identify priorities can enhance both communication and intimacy.

Paul, whom I met at a seminar in Chicago, said, "When my wife and I sat down and wrote our ten top priorities in life, I was surprised at how similar our lists were. We had been arguing a lot about little things and beginning to feel that we were incompatible. Focusing on our priorities brought us back to the basics and helped us focus on the really important things in life." Paul and his wife, Beverly, experienced the value of intentionally identifying priorities.

Setting Goals

Our priorities are stated in broad categories and indicate what we believe to be most important in life. Goals, on the other hand, are stepping stones that help us accomplish our priorities. For example, because I value my fellowship with God as most important and believe that it affects the quality of life in all other areas, I have chosen to set the goal of having a daily quiet time with God. This quiet time is an activity I believe will enhance my fellowship with God, keeping it alive and vital. Therefore, it is one of my goals. Another goal in this area is weekly attendance at a worship service, where I can sing praise to God and can hear the Scriptures explained and applied to life. Notice that both of these goals are measurable; that is, I can easily determine whether I accomplish these goals or fail to accomplish them, which is always the characteristic of a good goal.

If developing family relationships is one of my priorities, then my goals become specific statements of what would develop good family relationships. I might make a list that would look something like this:

1. A family vacation at least once a year
2. A daily devotional time with the family
3. Prayer with each child before going to bed
4. Each family member with certain household responsibilities, appropriate to age
5. A family forum once each week to share needs and struggles with the family

I might go on to list fifteen to twenty such goals that would develop good family relationships. Notice that each of these goals is specific enough to determine whether the goal is accomplished. For example, "I wish we got along better in our family" is not a well-defined goal. How would you know if you got along better? Goals should be measurable and attainable, not simply wishful thinking.

In most vocations, goal setting is standard fare. We are familiar with the concept, and we regularly set goals and seek to reach them. Many of us, however, have never set goals in our marriage relationship. If developing intimacy is one of our priorities, then the most practical way to accomplish that objective is to set realistic and measurable goals. To do so, we seek to answer these questions:

- What would enhance our marriage relationship?
- What would each of us like to see happen in our marriage?
- What are the kinds of activities that would keep our marriage alive?
- Would a daily sharing time enhance our relationship?
- How often would we like to go out to dinner?
- How often would we like to experience sexual intercourse?
- How often would we like to go on a weekend trip or take walks in the park?

Answering these kinds of questions will help us develop meaningful goals. Setting goals takes the vagueness out of reaching our priority concerns. Goal setting takes us from the realm of "I wish we had a good marriage" to the concrete steps that will give us a good marriage.

You may discover that you have difficulty agreeing on certain goals. For example, your spouse may wish to set a goal of having a daily sharing time seven days a week. You, on the other hand, may feel that this is unrealistic and that it would be far more feasible to set a goal of having a daily sharing time three or five days a week. In this case, it is important that each of you hear the other and be willing to negotiate, remembering that *some* progress is better than *no* progress. Often we must take small steps in marital growth before we can take larger steps.

Individuals who tend to be highly organized, highly motivated, and perfectionistic will tend to want all or nothing. They want to do everything by the book. They want to have a "perfect marriage," and sometimes have difficulty settling for anything less than 100 percent. In reality, most growth takes place slowly. We will create a much better growth environment if we express appreciation for the growth steps that our spouse is willing to take rather than condemning him/her for not doing more. None of us likes to be condemned; all of us appreciate genuine commendation. It is usually better to establish a smaller, realistic goal and rejoice in its accomplishment than to establish a larger, unattainable goal and feel that you are a failure because you did not reach it.

When the goal is unstated and exists only in the mind of one spouse, it does little except create conflict and disappointment; one spouse is working toward the goal while the other is totally unaware of the goal except as a demand from the spouse. When we jointly accept a goal as worthy of our time and energy, we are far more likely to accomplish it. It is highly possible that you and your spouse have never discussed and agreed upon a goal with regard to the frequency with which you would like to express love sexually. Each of you has an internal goal, but if the goal has not been shared and agreed upon, it will be a source of conflict. If you share individual goals and don't agree, then you can negotiate. A goal upon which we agree, though it may be more or less frequent than one of us would desire, is a step in the right direction.

The importance of goal setting cannot be overestimated. As you look back over your life, you will likely discover that most of your accomplishments grew out of goals you set for yourself. You may not have formulated them in writing, but in your mind you set a goal, and you worked to accomplish it. Those marriages that experience greatest intimacy are those marriages in which couples set specific, realistic, measurable goals and work toward the accomplishment of those goals. Clarifying goals helps each person work toward the goal.

Goals help couples get on the "same page" and work in harmony. I met Kathy at a marriage seminar in Sioux City, Iowa. I had been talking about the "five love languages." She identified her primary love language as "quality time." She felt most loved by her husband when the two of them could give their undivided attention to each other. At the end of our session she said to me, "When my husband and I established the goal of taking a walk together every Thursday evening after dinner, it changed my whole life. It was like we were dating again. Before this, I was beginning to feel unimportant to him. When I would ask him if he wanted to take a walk, he usually had something else to do. I felt rejected. Now he has our walk written on his calendar. We have missed only one week in three months, and that was because he was sick. I don't think the walk means as much to him as it does to me. That's what makes me feel so good; he is willing to do something that he knows makes me feel loved." Kathy and her husband, Bob, were reaping the benefits of setting goals.

ૐ ૐ ૐ

Clarifying priorities and setting realistic goals are effective ways of getting ready to stimulate marital growth. Without priorities and goals, your marriage will certainly change with the passing of time, but there may be little marital growth through the years.

I encourage you to establish a weekly planning session in which the two of you seek to clarify five to ten priorities in your lives. Then, over the next five to ten weeks, focus a session each week upon setting realistic goals related to accomplishing your priorities. A couple with a plan will accomplish far more growth than a couple who simply goes with the flow of life. As the old adage says, "Aim at nothing and you're sure to hit it."

If, as you read this suggestion, you are saying, "I don't have time for a weekly planning session," then the next chapter is specifically for you.

CHAPTER TWELVE

MAKING TIME
FOR THE IMPORTANT

Could it be that God did not understand how busy we were going to be? Otherwise, he would have made the day longer than twenty-four hours, or is it that we are trying to do more than he ever intended us to do? One night as my wife and I were driving home from church youth camp about 11:45, I remarked to her, "Somehow I don't think Jesus was ever this busy." As I read the Gospels, I see Jesus active but not hurried, accomplishing good but not appearing to be busy. I keep having the recurring thought that maybe he marched to the beat of a different drummer. Is it possible that we have been influenced more by our culture than by Christ and have substituted activity for accomplishment? There was a day when people had time to visit one another; when families had time to eat meals together; when families sat together at church; and when friends died, people had time to go to the funeral. Of course, those were the days before we had so many "time savers."

Washers, dryers, garage door openers, microwaves, personal computers, electric can openers, double ovens, sewing machines, remote controls, answering machines, and dishwashers—all designed to save us time. Ironic, isn't it? What have we done with all the time we have saved? Some sociologists feel that advanced technology has encouraged individuality and isolation, that we have turned our efforts toward becoming a success as an individual, and that we have lost the concept of succeeding as a family.

As Christians, we know that life's ultimate meaning is to be found in relationships: first, a relationship with God, and second, with people. On the human level, the marriage relationship is designed by God to be the most intimate, with the parent-child relationship a close second. Yet some of us are pursuing activities that have little to do with building marriage and family relationships. From time to time we have pangs of guilt but evidently not strongly enough to stop the merry-go-round and get off. If you feel the stress of such time pressure—and all of us do to some degree—then let me encourage you to read this chapter carefully.

There's little value in discussing time management until you have decided what you would like to accomplish in your marriage. If you have determined that your marriage relationship is one of your top priorities and you have set goals you would like to reach this week, this month, or this year, then you can start making time to accomplish these goals. Notice I said, "Making time." All of us have the same amount of time: 1,440 minutes per day. How we use it is up to us. You may be thinking, *I wish*. It may seem that people and situations dictate your use of time— your employer, your children, your church, your neighbors, and your leaking faucet. It is true that much of your time is already committed. However, these commitments are choices you made in the past. You chose the employment you presently have with its time schedule. You chose to have a sink, knowing that at times the faucet would leak, and you choose either to fix it yourself or to call a plumber.

Have you heard people say, "I know that I ought to . . . , but I just don't have time"? Have you made such statements yourself? Is it true that we don't have time to do what we ought to do? The word *ought* means to be bound by moral law, conscience, or a sense of duty. Is it possible that we don't have enough time to do the things that we are morally obligated to do? As Christians, I think our answer will be no.

We have time to do everything we ought to do. If we are not accomplishing our *oughts,* then we must examine our use of time. Ultimately, we can control the use of our time. The number-one barrier in failing to have time to reach our goals is over-commitment to activities that do not help us accomplish our goals. Managing time is simply a matter of utilizing our time to accomplish the things we believe we ought to do—our priorities and our goals.

The phrase *managing time* indicates that we have the responsibility for controlling our time. Often we are deluded into thinking that situations and other people control our time. As long as we live under such a delusion, we will live with unfulfilled goals and our priorities will be simply theoretical wishes. It is only as we manage our time that we will be able to accomplish our goals, reach our priority concerns, and invest our lives in the things we believe are really important.

The goals you have set for your marriage will require time. This time must come from the 1,440 minutes you have each day. If your goals are worthy and help you accomplish what you believe is really important in life, then they are worth the effort you will expend in managing your time so that you can accomplish those goals.

Analyzing Your Present Time Use

Let's get practical. If you really desire to accomplish the goals you have set, how much time will it take? I suggest that you put an approximate time beside each of your goals. For example, how much time do you want to spend in your daily sharing time?

The easiest way to find time to accomplish newly established goals is to look at your available free time, that time not already committed to a regularly scheduled activity. Some couples will say, "That's the problem. I don't have any free time." That brings me to my first suggestion. *Analyze your time use.* Some of us have an aversion to doing time studies in our vocations because we feel this is the way the supervisor checks up on us. But when we analyze our personal time, no one is checking up on us except ourselves. We are simply trying to become aware of how we spend our time so we can decide if we can make changes. It's our life. We are the ones who are managing our time; therefore, a personal time study should not be threatening.

One way to do this is to take a sheet of paper and, in the left-hand column, list the hours of the day. I suggest you start with midnight. Then in seven columns to the right, list the days of the week—Sunday through Saturday. Beside each hour of the day, note how you commonly use that time. Think through yesterday's activities. Starting with the time you awoke until the time you went to sleep, record what you did on the time chart. After you have done this individually, share your schedule with your spouse. If your goal is to have a fifteen-minute sharing time with each other, look for a time in which, if you make some modifications, you can accomplish your goal.

Getting in touch with how you presently use your time is the first step in making needed changes. Some people will find this time study much easier than others because some people's lives are more organized than others. For some, the time demands made upon them by vocation and other commitments are more predictable. The person with an 8:00 to 5:00 time commitment will find it easier to chart vocational time use than will the person whose vocational time commitment is pretty much of his/her own making. But the one with the more flexible vocational time commitment has more freedom in terms of creating quality "couple time" during the day.

Deciding What to Eliminate

A couple with six children was asked, "How do you do it all?" Their answer was, "We don't." The fact is that none of us can do it all. We have to decide which of the many good things we could be doing are the most important.

If your time study reveals that you have little uncommitted time, then your newly agreed upon goals will be more difficult to accomplish because you must eliminate something you are presently doing. Because we are creatures of habit, it is not always easy to eliminate activities to which we have grown accustomed. But if our goals and priorities are something "we ought to be doing," then surely we will make time to do them.

The key question to ask in deciding what to eliminate is, "What am I doing that is not in keeping with my stated priorities?" If you can answer that question, then you have identified things you can choose to eliminate. They may be wholesome, enjoyable activities, but if they are not helping you accomplish your goals in life, then perhaps you need to make some hard decisions.

When some couples record their daily schedules and begin looking for activities that are not helping them accomplish their goals, the most obvious culprit is the time they spend watching television. For some of these individuals, it is extremely difficult to reduce the time they watch TV. Unknowingly addicted to it, they feel uncomfortable, and perhaps even go through withdrawal, if they eliminate a significant amount of TV time. But it is important to eliminate marginal activities in order to do the things we have agreed are most important to us. The pain may be real, but the rewards will be satisfying. An intimate marriage relationship is far more exciting and fulfilling than anything you will ever see on television. I am not suggesting that anyone should totally eliminate TV time. For some people, watching TV is a means of unwinding after a hard day's work. However, if we spend all of our time unwinding, we may end up relaxed but have no time left for marriage building.

Sometimes we fall into excessive TV watching simply by default. Not much is going on in the marriage, so we sit in front of the tube. After awhile, we become friends with the TV characters and feel that we know them better than we know our spouse. To change will require an awareness of what has happened, a desire for greater intimacy in the marriage, and a willingness to make changes. Note that none of us will likely be successful at trying to force our spouse to cut back on TV watching. That choice must be made by the individual. Condemning statements about your spouse's TV habits will do little except drive a wedge between the two of you. It is far better to make good use of the time you do have together than to condemn your spouse because you don't have more.

Perhaps you will find that you have overcommitted yourself to good activities, even church activities, that are robbing time from your more important priorities. Your task is deciding "What good thing shall I eliminate so that I can do a better thing?" Let me encourage you not to rush out and drop these commitments tomorrow; that would be irresponsible. The Scriptures are firm on the importance of keeping our commitments (Ps. 15:4). However, most social and church commitments are for a defined period of time. You can look ahead and agree that when your present term as chairman of the good-deeds committee of the local civic club has ended, you will not accept that responsibility for another year. Once that activity ends, you will have additional time for your marriage relationship. A good solid commitment on the part of a spouse that he/she plans to eliminate some task three months down the road because of his desire to have more quality couple time will go a long way in creating a positive climate during the next three months. Most spouses are willing to wait for something that promises to enhance their marriage relationship.

Delegating Some of Your Responsibilities

Some couples could gain a significant amount of time by simply delegating specific responsibilities to children. Mother does not need to pick up or wash all the clothes. If children are tall enough to put clothes into the washer, they are old enough to operate it. Even toddlers can be taught to sort their clothes. In the process, you will not only gain additional time, but you will also train your children to take responsibility. Similarly, teenagers can mow lawns and do other household chores.

Some parents will say, "We have tried to give our children responsibility, but they will not accept it." My suggestion is a family forum once a week in which family members talk about improving family life. When children are given an opportunity to express freely their ideas and hear the ideas of parents, it creates an atmosphere where the children sense that they are a part of the family and thus have certain responsibilities. It has been my observation that couples who practice such a forum find far greater responsiveness on the part of their children than do those families where mothers and fathers simply give ultimatums as to what children are to do. If children can be a part of analyzing the various responsibilities that must be done around the house and have some input into what seems to them to be a fair and equitable distribution of responsibility, they are far more likely to accept this responsibility.

To parents who feel that they are not being good parents if they don't do everything for their children, let me remind you that responsible adults do not simply appear at age eighteen; they are grown over the first eighteen years. If children have not learned how to accept responsibility at home, they will not learn it as freshmen at the university. We do our children a great disservice when we do everything for them and make no requirements of them.

Some couples will object to the idea of delegating household responsibilities to children for this reason: "It takes more time to train them and get them to do it than it does to do it myself; thus, I am not saving time. It is actually taking more of my time." The problem here is the way parents have gone about delegating the responsibility. If in the family forum you have agreed on certain responsibilities for the child, you should also agree on the consequences if the child does not perform their responsibilities.

For example, if a teenager is given the responsibility of mowing the grass by noon on Saturday, the consequence for failing to do so might be to take away driving privileges for two days. This removes the necessity for the parent to spend time nagging the teenager about mowing the grass. The parent need never mention it again. If the teenager does not perform the task, then he simply suffers the consequences. Most teenagers will only fail to mow the grass by noon on Saturday one time. When they see that you are kind but firm in applying the consequence, they will learn responsibility. For some children, verbal compliments for a job well done are also extremely motivational.

Another means of delegation is hiring someone to do certain household and business related tasks, which will give us more time to invest in our marriage. A few years ago, we lost our lawn mower operator when our son went off to college. I had become accustomed to not having that responsibility. Rather than pick up that time commitment again, my wife and I agreed that it would be worth whatever it cost to hire someone to mow our grass and keep our lawn. Fortunately, lawn care companies have proliferated in our area the past few years. We found that it is really not too expensive. This decision saves me two hours a week.

In many families, a wife works outside the home and still continues to do all the meal preparation and housework. She finds herself thoroughly exhausted, with no time for meaningful conversation or sex. Perhaps some household responsibilities could be given to the husband. Most husbands would be willing to wash dishes and do laundry in order to have a more intimate relationship with their wives.

For wives only: if your husband assumes a new task around the house, which of the following statements would most likely be your response?

- Let him do it his way
- Criticize the way he does it
- Offer unsolicited advice
- Show gratitude
- Do something nice for him
- Nag if he doesn't do it properly

Delegating responsibility to a spouse, child, or a hired helper means that the task will not be done the way you would do it. Remember, the objective is not perfection but the creation of time to do the things you believe to be important.

Scheduling Ahead

By scheduling I don't mean what one wife tried. Her husband was overly involved in work and other activities. It had been a long time since they had lunch or dinner together. Without telling him, she got his appointment book and wrote her name for a 12:00 lunch on Thursday. A few days later, she found that her name had been crossed out and a business appointment added. He never said a word to her. Such backdoor efforts are usually counterproductive.

I am talking about a front door approach in which the two of you sit down with your calendars and find a day when you can schedule quality couple time. It may be a meal together, a walk in the park, a picnic, or a weekend trip together. It needs to be something different from the ordinary. If most of us do not schedule such activities ahead of time, they will not happen. Many couples have found that scheduling a weekly date is the only way they can spend regular quality time with each other. It requires discipline, but it says, "This is a priority for us." We normally do what we schedule.

Some may find it offensive to think of *scheduling* time with their spouse. They believe that a marriage should be spontaneous. However, in our highly regimented society, if we do not schedule quality time with our spouse for communication, for sexual involvement, for discussion of issues, and for solving problems, we will likely accomplish our goals only sporadically. Scheduling should not be viewed as negative but as positive. The fact that our spouse cares enough to schedule this activity or this quality time together is emotionally encouraging. We can still be spontaneous in the way we use our scheduled time. The purpose of the schedule is to make sure the time is available.

I remember the wife who said to me, "I had a real aversion to scheduling our sexual relationship. I had always thought that was the one part of life that should be truly spontaneous. But when I realized that it had been three months since we had made love, it dawned on me that spontaneity was not working. Now that we have scheduled our times to be together, we are both much more creative in preparing ourselves and each other for this time of lovemaking." Whatever the goal, scheduling time to do it increases the possibility that it will actually be done.

Encouraging Time Alone

In emphasizing quality couple time, don't overlook the fact that each of us needs quality time alone—time to think, pray, and reflect on life. It is only as we are personally enriched that we will be able to enrich each other. Couples need to cooperate in helping each other have such time for personal reflection.

The Scriptures often record that Jesus went aside and spent time alone (Mark 1:35; Luke 4:42; 5:16). If it was important for him, it is no less important for us. To keep ourselves alive emotionally, spiritually, and physically, all of us need time alone—time to reflect, to think, to read, to walk, to smell the roses, to pray, or to do other activities we find meaningful and revitalizing.

This may mean volunteering to keep the children in order to give your spouse some time apart. It may mean encouraging him/her to leave the household tasks undone in order to spend time doing something he/she really wants to do. All of us need such times alone. Couples who encourage each other and help each other find time for such solitary experiences will enhance their couple time when they are together.

ᨀ ᨀ ᨀ

Our emphasis in the last two chapters has been on overcoming time barriers to building communication and intimacy. However, we are all aware that sometimes what we call time barriers are really emotional barriers. We say, "I don't have time," but in reality there are emotional reasons why we don't want to spend time together. We may be angry because of some action of the spouse, or we may be afraid of intimacy, so we stay on the run. As one wife said, "As long as I am on the run, it is hard for him to talk to me, hug me, or get close to me." No amount of time management will deal with these emotional problems. These we will discuss in the chapters that follow.

CHAPTER THIRTEEN

IDENTIFYING
OUR DIFFERENCES

B efore Brett got married he dreamed about how wonderful it would be to get up every morning and have breakfast with his wife, Allyson. After he got married, he found out that Allyson didn't do mornings. He dreamed of hiking and overnight camping, but he discovered that the Holiday Inn was her idea of overnight camping. He believed in saving money. In fact, he paid cash for the ring (it was a discreetly small one). Her philosophy was "Shop today; you may be sick tomorrow." Brett believed there was a rational answer for everything. "Now let's think about this" was his favorite statement. "I'm tired of thinking. Why can't we just for once do what we want to do without thinking about it?" was Allyson's response.

Opposites Attract

Most of us can identify with Brett and Allyson. The way we think, act, and approach life in general is quite different from our spouse. In fact, some would say, "We differ on almost everything. We are like night and day. We're not sure how we ever got together." Not all of us see our differences quite so profoundly, but most of us can readily identify a number of areas in which we are quite different from our spouse.

Many of our differences were established in the process of growing up, as we discussed in chapter 6. We observed our parents, who served as role models, and we either identified with them by responding to life in a similar way or we deliberately chose to respond to life in an opposite way, reacting to what we felt was negative. Each of us developed a unique pattern of responding to life emotionally, socially, intellectually, and spiritually.

Differences are also rooted in the fact that we are creatures of God. God is infinitely creative. No two of his creatures are exactly alike. We are God-made originals. He made us unique so that we would complement each other. Thus, in our dating we were attracted to someone different from ourselves. She was outgoing; he was shy. He was a hard worker; she was fun loving. He was a spender and bought her nice things, which made her feel special because she tended to pinch every penny. Opposites attract. In the dating process, we tend to be drawn to persons who complement our personality.

Some of our differences are rooted in the roles society teaches males and females. For example, Western society has taught men to hold in their emotions, while women are encouraged to give free expression to their feelings. Research has shown that American men and women tend to follow this cultural pattern. However, the fact that there are thousands of men and women who do not fit the pattern indicates that this is not a gender-related characteristic but one taught by the culture.

In summary, our differences grow out of the fact that we are creatures of an infinitely creative God, that we grew up in unique family environments, that we were taught cultural and sexual roles, and that we are influenced by our unique genetic composition.

I cannot predict the specific differences you will discover in your marriage, but I can predict that the differences will emerge. In this chapter, I want to share some of the differences I have observed as I have counseled couples over the past thirty years. I think you will be able to identify with some of these.

Morning Persons and Night Persons

When James got married, he had the idea that about 10:30 each evening he and Susan would go to bed together, sometimes making love and sometimes simply enjoying each other's presence in bed. Susan, however, had never dreamed of going to bed at 10:30. In fact, her prime time was from 10:00 P.M. to midnight. That is when she enjoyed reading, painting, playing games, doing anything that demanded a lot of energy. Susan is representative of night people. The world is full of them—male and female. Very often they are married to a morning person, whose motor turns off at 10:00 P.M. and cranks back up at 6:00 A.M. While the morning person awakes with the enthusiasm of a kangaroo, springing to face the day with excitement, the night person hides under the covers and thinks, *They must be playing a game. No one could be that excited in the morning.*

Before marriage, the person whose motor turned off at 10:00 P.M. was charged up by the excitement of the night person. James said, "Susan is the only person who was ever able to keep me awake after 10:00 P.M. That's why I knew I must be in love with her." Before marriage, Susan had told James, "Don't call me in the morning; that is not my time of day." James had lovingly complied with this request, never knowing how grumpy Susan could be before noon.

Dead Seas and Babbling Brooks

If you are familiar with the geography of Israel, you know that the Sea of Galilee flows south by way of the Jordan River into the Dead Sea. The Dead Sea goes nowhere. Many of us have that kind of personality. We can receive all kinds of thoughts, feelings, and experiences throughout the day. We have a large reservoir where we store it all, and we are perfectly happy not to talk. In fact, if you say to a Dead Sea, "What's wrong? Why aren't you talking tonight?" the Dead Sea will likely say, "Nothing's wrong. What makes you think something's wrong?" The Dead Sea is being perfectly honest. He/she is content not to talk.

At the other extreme is the Babbling Brook. These are individuals for whom whatever comes into the eye gate or the ear gate comes out the mouth gate—usually in less than sixty seconds. Whatever these people see, whatever they hear, they tell. In fact if no one is at home, they will call someone on the telephone: "Do you know what I just saw? Do you know what I just heard?" They have no reservoir. Whatever they experience, they talk about.

Often a Dead Sea will marry a Babbling Brook. Before the marriage, the differences are viewed as attractive. For example, while dating, the Dead Sea can relax. He or she does not have to think, *How will I get the conversation started tonight?* or *How can I keep things flowing?* All they have to do is to sit there, nod their head, and say, "Uh huh." The Babbling Brook will fill up the evening. The Babbling Brook, on the other hand, finds the Dead Sea equally attractive because Dead Seas are the world's best listeners. Five years after marriage, however, the Babbling Brook may be saying, "We've been married five years and I don't know him/her." At the same time, the Dead Sea is saying, "I know him/her too well. I wish they would stop the flow and give me a break."

The Neatnik and the Slob

"I've never known anyone as sloppy as Barry," said Meredith. How many wives have said this about their husbands less than a year after their wedding? Interestingly, before marriage this never bothered Meredith. Oh, she may have noticed that the car was sometimes dirty or that his apartment was not as neat as she would have had it. But somehow she concluded, "Barry is a more relaxed person than I. That's good; I like that. I need to loosen up a little." Barry, on the other hand, looked at Meredith and found an angel. "Isn't it wonderful that Meredith is so neat? Now I don't have to worry about keeping everything clean because she will take care of that." Three years later, however, he is being bombarded with verbal stones of condemnation, to which he responds, "I don't understand why you would get so upset over a few dirty socks."

Aggressive Persons and Passive Persons

The old adage says, "Some people read history; others make it." Usually these people are married to each other. The aggressive husband or wife believes that each day is a new opportunity to advance the cause. Whatever they want, whatever they believe right, they are out to make it happen. They will go to all ends, they will turn every stone, and they will do everything humanly possible to accomplish their goals in life. On the other hand, the passive spouse sits by analyzing, thinking, wondering *what if?* and waiting for something good to happen.

Before marriage, these traits attracted the two individuals to each other. The aggressive partner found it marvelous to observe how calm, cool, and collected his/her future spouse could be in the midst of life's experiences. How secure and stable the loved one was! The passive person was enamored by the activity of the aggressive partner and was pleased to have someone make plans and chart courses for their future. Now, after marriage, the couple often finds these same traits difficult to live with. The aggressive partner keeps trying to push the passive partner into action, while the passive partner keeps saying, "It's going to be all right. Don't get so excited. Everything's going to work out."

Organized and Spontaneous

In this marriage, one partner is organized and the other is spontaneous. The Organizer takes weeks preparing for a vacation—looking at the map, charting the route, calling ahead for reservations, planning, and packing. The Spontaneous Spouse waits until the night before and says, "Why don't we go to the coast instead of the mountains? The sun is so beautiful, and the weather is wonderful." This sends the Organizer into a tail spin, and the vacation becomes torture.

Before marriage, Tricia was impressed with her husband Trent's organizational skills: "You balance your checkbook every month? That's wonderful!" After marriage, however, she is asking, "You want me to record *every* check I write? That's impossible. No one does that." Trent, of course, quickly shows her his checkbook—with every check accurately recorded.

The Professor and the Dancer

For the Professor, everything must be reasoned out: "We must have logical reasons for doing everything we do. If it is not logical, we shouldn't do it." The Dancer is intuitive: "We don't need logical reasons for everything we do. We do some things simply because we enjoy them. I don't know why. Do I always have to know why? I want to do it just because." Before marriage, the Professor was proud of the Dancer, as was the Dancer of the Professor. Too often after the marriage, however, the Professor is slowly driven insane by the same illogical behavior, and the Dancer wonders how he/she can continue living with a person so obsessed with reason.

"Ellen, listen to me. The walls are not dirty; they don't need painting again. Don't you understand that?" to which Ellen responds, "Yes, I understand that, but I don't want pea green walls any longer." The Professor has a difficult time making decisions based on desire. The Dancer cannot imagine why anyone would want to be held in the prison of logic.

The Reader and the TV Addict

The Reader will never understand how anyone can waste so much time watching TV, while the TV Addict deplores the silent withdrawal of the Reader. Rob said, "Why can't we enjoy a TV show together? Why do you always have to sit around reading a book? We could have fun if you'd watch some things with me." Grace responds, "I'll never watch that junk. It's a waste of time. I use my mind when I read."

Rob and Grace are illustrating a whole category of differences related to interests. Instead of TV, it may be movies, yard work, computers, exercise, or any number of other activities. When spouses have different interests, sometimes one is unwilling to understand or accept the value of the other person's pursuits. The symphony lover says, "Bravo, Bravo. Don't you just love that Opus no. 12 in A Minor?" to which the bluegrass devotee responds, "You call that stuff music?" The jogger says, "My goal is the marathon. Rain or shine, I'll be running," whereas the walker says, "I don't want to ruin my knees by jogging. I want to enjoy the scenery as I walk."

Coach or First Class

The First Class thinker always wants the best of everything—the best shirt or dress, the most expensive of whatever. The Coach thinker looks for a bargain. The difference often arises when they are buying a car. One will want the extras; the other, the basics. When they go out to eat, fast food is fine with the Coach. After all, a burger is a burger. However, the First Class person would never eat a burger unless it were served on a crystal plate.

When they travel, one thinks economy is fine; the other has in mind the elegant. The Coach wants to squirrel money away for the future, while the First Class thinker isn't sure there will be a future: "Let's enjoy the present."

Before marriage, the Coach was enamored with the money the First Class spouse spent to make them happy, while the First Class thinker appreciated the conservative nature of the spouse-to-be. After marriage, however, the Coach lives in fear of bankruptcy, while the First Class spouse is tired of the lectures on economy.

"I wish that just once you would order something that is not the cheapest thing on the menu," said Philip. His wife, Gail, responded, "I thought you would be proud of me for saving money." "It makes me feel like you think I'm a failure . . . like I can't afford to buy you something nice," said Philip. "I never knew you felt that way," said Gail. "Waiter," she said, raising her hand, "change mine to a filet mignon."

Sunday-Morning and Wednesday-Night Christians

The Wednesday night crowd at church is much smaller than the Sunday morning crowd. We accept this as a way of life in the church. The problem comes when you are a Wednesday-Night Christian married to a Sunday-Morning Christian. You cannot understand how any Christian could be satisfied to go to church only on Sunday mornings, while the Sunday-Morning Christian feels that only a religious fanatic would go to church as often as you do.

The Wednesday-Night Christian often feels that he/she is more spiritually mature than their spouse. While this may be true in individual cases, it certainly is not true across the board. Who is more spiritually mature—the person who goes to church only on Sunday morning but has a consistent, daily quiet time with God and consistently applies the Bible to daily life, praying throughout the day and walking in fellowship with Christ; or the person who goes to church Sunday morning, Sunday night, and Wednesday night but has no consistent quiet time with God, is not involved in intercessory pray throughout the week, and in fact, does not enjoy God's fellowship between services. The answer is obvious.

Some will object that this illustration is going to the extreme. However, many pastors will bear testimony that some Wednesday-Night Christians are people who have tremendous emotional needs, so they come to church on Wednesday night to gain support. They are not mature Christians but Christians who have not yet learned to apply biblical truth as a way of life. Do not hear this as an attempt to discourage Wednesday night attendance but, instead, to indicate that this difference is not necessarily a matter of spiritual maturity versus immaturity.

As Christians we often take pride in feeling that "God is on my side." If I can convince myself that reading is more spiritual than watching television, then I can blast my spouse who happens to be a watcher rather than a reader. If I can convince myself that any child of God should always go first class, then I can clobber my spouse as being less spiritually mature for wanting to travel economy class. However, it is not a matter of reading being more spiritual than watching television. The question is, what am I reading (or what am I watching), and how does this activity affect my relationship with God and my ministry to others. It is not that flying first class is always God's will for his children. The question is a matter of stewardship. Each of us will differ in our preferences, but we must all put our preferences under the lordship of Christ.

ᓫ ᓫ ᓫ

The differences we have discussed in this chapter are not meant to provide an exhaustive list but are simply samples of differences commonly seen in marriages. I would encourage making a list of differences you observe in your marriage. The chart on the next page, containing some differences we have talked about as well as others, may help you get started. The purpose of this chapter is to help you identify the differences. In the next chapter we will discuss how to make these differences an asset rather than a liability.

Personality Opposites

1.	**Dead Sea** Stores thoughts and feelings. Talks little.	**Babbling Brook** Tells all. Whatever they hear, see, or think, they tell.
2.	**Robin** Rises early, alert and singing. "The early bird gets the worm."	**Owl** Awake at night but come morning, the "do not disturb" sign is on the door.
3.	**Aggressive** "Let's go get it." "Let's make it happen." "Seize the day."	**Passive** "Let's wait till it comes to us." "Everything comes to him who waits."
4.	**Neatnik** "A place for everything and everything in its place" is their theme.	**Slob** "Where is it?" is their most asked question.
5.	**Planner** Plans ahead. Takes care of every detail.	**Spontaneous Doer** "Don't waste time planning. We'll work out the details as we go."
6.	**The Butterfly** Flits from event to event. Life's a party.	**The Raccoon** "Can't we stay home tonight? I'm tired."
7.	**The Professor** "Let's be logical." "Think about it."	**The Dancer** "I don't know why, I just do." "Why do I have to have a reason?"
8.	**First Class** "It only costs five dollars more to go first class. We deserve it."	**Economy** "We can save lots of money, and economy is nice enough."
9.	**Reader** "Why would anyone waste time watching TV when there are so many good books to read?"	**TV Addict** "It's my way of relaxing." "I don't like to read." "Besides, I don't watch that much TV."
10.	**Symphony Lover** "Bravo, Bravo." "Don't you just love that Opus no. 12 in A minor?"	**Blue Grass Devotee** "Now that's real music; it tells a story." "Listen to that banjo."
11.	**The Jogger** The aerobic exercise—jogging. "My goal is the marathon. Rain or shine, I'll be there."	**The Walker** "I don't want to ruin my knees by jogging. I want to enjoy the scenery as I walk."
12.	**Channel Surfer** "Why waste time on commercials. I can watch three shows at once if I omit the commercials."	**Commercial Watcher** "Can't we just enjoy one program instead of seeing parts of three? Besides, we can talk during the commercial."

CHAPTER FOURTEEN

MAKING DIFFERENCES
AN ASSET

Differences can be deadly. They can also be delightful. Recently I discovered my wife in the kitchen at 7:00 A.M. This had not happened since the last child went off to college. First, I hit my head on the cabinet door that she had opened, and then I rammed my elbow into the microwave door she had opened. I turned to get a knife to cut my grapefruit, and in doing so, I almost tackled her. I apologized and then said, with all sincerity, "You know, darling, I am really glad that you are not a morning person." I suddenly realized how my attitude had changed from the early days when I resented that she didn't bounce out of bed like I did every morning. I realized how much I had come to enjoy eating breakfast with God (he is always awake). I enjoy the predictability that the only cabinet doors that will be open are the ones I open, and the only drawers that will be open are the ones I open. I had not only come to accept our differences; I was actually delighting in the differences.

Unity, Not Uniformity

Why do you suppose Jesus chose twelve men with different personalities to serve as his disciples? I believe it was because he did not desire uniformity but, rather, unity—where each complemented the other as they worked together as a team to accomplish God's purposes. Likewise, in marriage there is a vast difference between unity and uniformity. It is God's purpose that we become one, but it is never God's desire that we become alike. The differences are there so that we complement each other and strengthen our effectiveness in serving Christ.

Unfortunately, in the real world of marriage, differences have often driven couples near delirium. Surely *this* is not God's intention. Differences are part of our humanity. There will never be a married couple with no differences. The key is to make our differences an asset rather than a liability. There are constructive steps we can take to make our differences work for us rather than against us.

Turning Differences into Assets

In the last chapter, we emphasized identifying differences. You probably discovered that you are very different from your spouse in certain personality and behavioral patterns. Now the second step is to identify which of those differences are troublesome for you. In certain areas, you have already learned to live in harmony with your differences. For instance, if you like to cook and your spouse likes to wash dishes, it is easy to delight in your differences. But what are the differences that lead to arguments? What are the differences that continue to irritate you?

Once you identify a difference, answer the following question: What is it about this difference that disturbs me? For example, let's say that you are a morning person and your spouse is a night person, and this difference has been a significant struggle for you. As a morning person, ask yourself, "What is it about this difference that disturbs me?" Perhaps you will find that you sense condemnation from your spouse when you face the morning enthusiastically. Maybe you feel guilty when you go to bed early and are not able to continue activities with your spouse. Maybe you discover that you feel resentment toward your spouse because he/she will not get up early and walk with you as you see other spouses doing. Perhaps you resent having to be quiet so as not to disturb him/her or having to prepare your own breakfast when, in your mind, a good spouse would be doing that for you. Or maybe you resent having to eat your breakfast alone instead of having someone with whom you can share the first meal of the day. The more you can clarify what disturbs you, the better equipped you will be to process that difference and to find an answer to your dilemma.

One husband said, "I'm aggressive; my wife is passive. I can accept that, but what bothers me is that at work she doesn't speak up for herself. I feel like she allows her supervisor to use her as a doormat, and that bothers me." Identifying those things you find irritating or troublesome is a positive step in the process of learning to delight in our differences.

A further step is answering the questions, "Why does that disturb me? What is there about me, about my history, about my belief system, that causes me to be irritated with my spouse's behavior?" Most of the time the answers to these questions are found in our past. We were brought up to think a certain way, to respond a certain way; thus, when we discover that our marriage partner does not agree with our beliefs, thoughts, and behavior patterns, we find ourselves frustrated. Until we analyze ourselves, however, these reasons may be hidden in our subconscious. When I better understand myself and why I find certain things irritating, I am better able to reveal the source of my feelings to my spouse. Such understanding creates a climate for talking about our differences and finding new ways of responding.

For example, the aggressive husband discussed above may discover that he was raised by an aggressive mother or father who communicated clearly that in order to be valuable you must be aggressive. "If you let people walk on you, you are a nobody" is the emotional message deeply written within. With such a background, it is easy to see why this person is irritated. They don't want to be married to a "nobody." The issue is really their own self-esteem. Such insight prepares the way for meaningful dialog with the spouse as opposed to surface arguments that seldom lead anywhere.

The question is, "Why does this bother me?" Perhaps you are bothered by your spouse's taste for expensive things because you were reared to be frugal, and you feel that it is almost sinful to spend so much money. Perhaps you were raised in a poor family in which you lacked the essentials of life, and you now live in fear that the same will happen to you and your children if you are not frugal. On the other hand, perhaps such display of expensive items causes you guilt because you feel others will interpret it as a display of materialism. The answer to why a difference with your spouse bothers you can be answered only by you—for only you can discover your inner feelings, which grow from your history and personality.

Once you have analyzed your own thoughts and feelings about what irritates you and why, you are ready to talk with your spouse. Remember, one of the keys in good communication is using "I" statements instead of "you" statements. The purpose is to explain to your spouse your understanding of why you find their behavior to be troublesome. It is essential that you allow each other to be human—to have differences and to have feelings that arise from those differences.

Since the beginning of their marriage, Robert had found it irritating that his wife was unwilling to go to bed with him at what he called "a reasonable hour." When she insisted on watching television or reading a book until midnight, he found it extremely painful. "I understood staying up until midnight when we were dating; it was so we could be together. But now we are married, and she doesn't want to be with me," Robert said. His wife, Jill, was greatly annoyed by the sense of condemnation she felt from him. When Robert began to analyze his problem, he discovered that the real reason he was annoyed had nothing to do with her staying up later; rather, it grew out of his own sense of being unloved by Jill because his sexual needs were not being met. When he was able to share this with her in an open, accepting conversation, then they were able to clarify that the solution lay not in her changing from a night person to a morning person but in finding a way to meet sexual needs. She continued to be a night person and he continued to be a morning person, but when sexual needs were met and his emotional need for love was satisfied, he did not go to bed with resentment but with gratitude for a wife who loved him even though they were different. The process of clarifying and analyzing your differences enables you to talk about them in a new light and to focus on the things that need attention rather than on condemning each other.

Difficulties that have developed from differences can be resolved. Unfortunately, some couples have invested all their energy in trying to change each other so that they have no differences. This is almost never successful. If we accept the differences, stop condemning each other for being different, and focus instead on the difficulties that have arisen from our differences, then we can find resolution. We will both feel accepted as persons and not condemned for being who we are.

The process I have described is not easy. However, Christians have outside help. Jesus once said, "You can do nothing without Me" (John 15:5). Some of us have tried hard to keep our differences from dividing us, but we have been unsuccessful. We need God's wisdom if we are to understand and utilize our differences in a constructive way. The Scriptures encourage us to ask for help: "If any of you lacks wisdom, he should ask God, who gives to all generously and without criticizing, and it will be given to him" (James 1:5). Most of us admit that we need wisdom—a new way of looking at our differences. Before you continue reading, perhaps you will want to pause and ask God to use this chapter to help you work through the differences you have never been able to resolve.

Hopefully an open conversation with your spouse will lead you to verbally accept each other's differences, removing the spirit of condemnation and strife and creating a spirit of friendliness. When you say, "I am willing to accept the fact that I am a morning person and you are a night person and that one is not better than another," you have taken a giant step in making difficulties a delight. Now that you are friends looking for solutions, you are open to the possibility of making adjustments that will make the differences less irritating. "How can I adjust to make life easier for you?" is a good question with which to begin. Give each other specific suggestions. For example, the Owl might suggest to the Robin that he/she wait until they get out of the bedroom before singing, "Oh, What a Beautiful Morning." To make progress, we must be willing to make adjustments. We are not changing our basic orientation; we are willingly changing our behavior to make life easier for our spouse.

Ultimately, we hope to discover the assets in our differences. How can this difference become a positive thing in our marriage? For example, the Raccoon will get exposed to much more of life if he/she will see the value of the Butterfly's spontaneous spirit. Following the Butterfly will lead the Raccoon into many exciting experiences he/she would never have known. On the other hand, the Butterfly might learn to relax and enjoy serenity if he/she will see the value of a quiet evening at home. We all need time with others, time alone, and time with our spouse. The Raccoon and the Butterfly can enhance each other's lives, which is God's purpose for differences. Acknowledging the assets rather than cursing the differences leads to delighting in the differences.

One of the great prayer promises in the Bible is found in 1 John 5:14: "Now this is the confidence we have before Him: whenever we ask anything according to His will, He hears us." Praying in keeping with the will of God gives us great assurance that God will answer our prayers. When we ask God to help us identify and make the most of our differences, we are definitely praying in the will of God. It is God's desire that we learn to make our differences an asset to our marriage.

This is illustrated by the Christian church. In 1 Corinthians 12, Paul indicates that God has given individual Christians different gifts or abilities. He indicates that these gifts are given "for the common good" (v. 7 NIV). That is, the spiritual gifts that God has given to each Christian are for the common good of the whole Body. We are not all alike; our abilities differ, but each of us is to play a vital role in the one Body of Christ. Our differences are to be complementary. We work together as one unit, allowing each gifted Christian to perform his or her role in the church.

A Christian marriage is to follow the same pattern. We are to recognize our differences as gifts from God and seek to allow each person to utilize his/her unique personality for the benefit of the marriage. When we pray for God's help in this process, we are praying according to his will, and we know that he hears us and will answer us.

Our request in prayer is that God will help us understand and accept our spouse's differences as we discover ways that our differences can be an asset to our marriage. We are not praying that God will change our spouse and make him/her like us. We are praying for God's help in discussing the difficulties our differences have caused, and we are asking for divine help in finding harmony.

Paul's admonition in Romans 15:7 needs to be heard: "Accept one another, just as the Messiah also accepted you, to the glory of God." Accepting one another with our differences is a major step in both spiritual growth and marital growth.

Can differences really be delightful? Ask Spontaneous Charles and Mary the Planner. "In the early years, our vacations were disasters," said Charles. "She was on my back for months to make motel reservations and get tickets to attractions. I never did. My idea was to get in the car, start driving, and let the billboards be your guide. If anything is worth seeing, it will be on a billboard. When night comes, get a motel. Don't bother with reservations. If they want your money, they will make a room. 'No Vacancy' signs? They are only on the cheap places. I don't want to stay there anyway." He continued, "I hate to admit it, but in those days we would often be looking for a room well after midnight, both of us tired, irritable, and in no mood for sex. I can't believe we called it a vacation.

"Now we have real vacations. Mary works on the plans for a year. She gets all the travel books and chooses good hotels at the best prices. They even know our names when we check in. My job? To come up with three spontaneous events throughout the week. I love it. That's my cup of tea. You wouldn't believe the things we've done: hang gliding at Nags Head, dogsledding in Alaska, skinny-dipping at midnight—real vacations. No more wasting time looking for a motel where we can argue. Oh yes, we are delighting in our differences."

Or ask Kathy, the disorganized musician, about her differences with Peter, the neatnik engineer. "Throughout my adult life, I have never been able to keep up with my car keys. When I was single, I must have lost my keys or locked them in the car at least twenty times. My father, who is the most patient man in the world, always kept four sets of my keys on hand at all times. I called night or day, and he would come to my rescue with a fresh set of keys.

"In the first year of my marriage, I lost my keys seven times. We had to have the house locks rekeyed each time because the house key was with the car keys. Peter was beside himself. He gave me lectures; he told me to carry an extra key in my bra. I couldn't remember that either. I really thought he was going to divorce me over my keys. I felt terrible about myself. I knew I should be more responsible, but I honestly didn't know what to do.

"One night, I told Peter that I knew that this was one of my weaknesses (that was putting it mildly) and that I really needed his help. I asked him to put his engineering mind to work and help me find a solution. I am amazed at what happened. First, he traded my car for one with those electronic buttons on the outside of the door so you don't have to have a key to get inside. I don't have any trouble remembering numbers because I'm a musician. Then he mounted my car keys to a tennis ball. I agreed that I would never take the keys out of the car. Who wants to carry a tennis ball in your purse? I always drop the tennis ball on the floor; it's really easy to find when I get back inside. As for the house key, every morning when Peter leaves the house, he puts the key in a 'secret place.' He *never* forgets. I get it every afternoon when I get home and immediately put it back in the 'secret place.' If I happen to forget, Peter has six extra house keys. Last year, I only forgot three times. He says that's great.

"I guess Peter still wishes I were more organized, but he enjoys my music and he knows that creativity and disorganization sometimes go together. I'm sure glad I'm married to him. I'd hate to be married to someone like me. We would spend half our lifetime looking for our keys. Oh yes! Peter and I delight in our differences."

๛ ๛ ๛

Every difference has the potential for delight. If we really believe that God's intention is that our differences will be complementary, we will look for and experience those delights. One troublesome difference that deserves special attention is "defensive reactions." Why do you and your spouse sometimes react defensively to each other? In chapter 15, I hope you will find the answer.

CHAPTER FIFTEEN

WHY DO I GET SO DEFENSIVE?

Defensiveness is not something we create; it is something we observe. It happens. My wife and I can be having a perfectly wonderful evening, with the conversation flowing freely and both of us feeling relaxed as we enjoy a few leisure moments. Yet my wife might say or do something, and I suddenly find myself getting defensive. Something happens inside me; it is as though my emotions jump to attention, like soldiers preparing to defend a strategic position. These emotional soldiers bark out orders, and my response to my wife will be designed to keep her from further penetrating that area of my life. I might change the subject, diverting the conversation to a more acceptable arena. On the other hand, I may respond with verbal gunfire designed to stop further discussion of the matter. I may even retreat to another room and hope she doesn't pursue. Whatever my response, the leisure time is over; the pleasant conversation has ended. We have gone from being allies to being enemies. We did not consciously set out to change our pleasant pasture to a brutal battlefield. It simply happened. Are we then pawns to these internal emotional monsters that drive us to a defensive mode, thereby destroying conversation and intimacy? The thesis of this chapter is that we can come to understand these defensive responses, learn something about ourselves from them, and find ways to defuse their destructiveness.

Causes of Defensive Attitudes

Why are we so fast to defend ourselves? To defend is to protect and oppose. Thus, when we are defensive, we are *protecting something* and *opposing someone*. Defensive behavior is a barrier to communication. Consider the following encounter between Bev and Jim.

"Your tie is crooked," Bev said to her husband, Jim, as he left the house. To this Jim responded sarcastically, "So, what other good news do you have for me today?"

"I was just trying to help," answered Bev.

"I don't know how I ever made it before I married you," Jim said angrily as he slammed the door.

"Why did he get so defensive?" wondered Bev. "All I said was 'Your tie is crooked.' I just wanted him to look nice when he got to work."

Defensiveness stops constructive communication dead in its tracks. The conversation is over, and we are not likely to bring up the subject again. Such defensiveness is a barrier to our oneness, a wedge between us. Neither of us is happy about it, but we seem helpless to keep defensive responses from occurring. When they do, we always feel badly about our relationship.

Self-Esteem Issues

Why do we respond so immediately and passionately when our spouse says certain things? The most common reason is that our self-esteem has been threatened by our spouse's comments.

Eric was chopping onions, and Jennifer was pouring oil in the pan. When Eric left to adjust the radio station, his wife plopped the onions in the oil. He returned and suggested, "You know there's a better way to do that?"

To this, Jennifer responded, "Why do you always have to be in charge of everything?"

"I just thought you would want my advice. You know this meal is my specialty," Eric said.

"Then cook your special meal," she snorted as she walked out of the kitchen, leaving him wondering, "How did this happen?" He was simply going to tell Jennifer that she should have heated the oil before she added the onions. Because of her defensiveness, he never got around to giving his valuable advice, and the evening was ruined for both of them.

What happened in this kitchen adventure? His statement touched one of her emotional hot spots. All of us have them. Like the dentist pick that touches an exposed nerve, sending pain throughout the body, words can touch an emotional nerve, and the whole mind and body respond defensively. This is not a reasoned response but an involuntary response. We don't know that it is going to happen until it has happened. We are sometimes surprised ourselves that we were so defensive.

These emotional hot spots are directly tied to our self-esteem and find their root in our personal histories. The particular emotional hot spots differ with each individual. One husband may become defensive when his wife makes a suggestion about his cooking. Another husband simply accepts her suggestion. One wife becomes defensive when her husbands says, "The speed limit is fifty-five," while another wife might say, "Thanks, I didn't know I was speeding."

In the previous illustration, I discovered that Eric's mother was a master cook (according to Eric). Eric himself had considerable culinary skills and was very methodical in his preparation of food. Jennifer viewed herself as a highly competent person, but her self-image was threatened by Eric's statement in the kitchen. The message she heard was that she was incompetent.

The more passionate the defensive response, the more deeply self-worth has been threatened. George was driving down the interstate with Jan, anticipating a good vacation together, when she said, "The speed limit is sixty-five."

George came to an abrupt halt on the side of the road, got out of the van, and said, "OK, you drive. I'm not spending this vacation listening to you tell me how to drive."

When Jan didn't move, he repeated, "Come on. You drive."

Jan responded, "I don't want to drive."

George shouted, "You're going to drive or keep your mouth shut." After some silence, he said, "I don't know why our vacations always have to be like this."

Such an extreme defensive reaction to one statement almost certainly indicates that George's self-worth has been deeply threatened. He wants to see himself as a responsible adult, but he interprets Jan's statement as a put-down. The feeling is almost unbearable. He desperately wants her approval and appreciation, which make him feel good about himself. When he gets what he interprets as condemnation instead of approval, he becomes extremely defensive.

What Jan did not know is that George's father had been extremely critical of his driving when he was a teenager, warning him constantly about speeding. In fact, George had two accidents, both of which came from speeding. When Jan said "The speed limit is 65," she touched George's emotional hot spot relating to these memories. George heard the message clearly: "You are not a good driver, you are irresponsible, and you will probably have an accident."

Typically, we feel justified in our defensive behavior. After thought, we may not like our response, but we almost always believe that we had a right to be defensive. We like to remind ourselves of Jesus' righteous anger when he threw the money changers out of the temple. It seems justified to us because the other person had no right to strike us where it hurts so deeply. The problem is, our spouses have no idea they are touching an emotional hot spot.

Jan was simply trying to keep her husband from getting a speeding ticket and, thus, putting a damper on their vacation. It was only afterward that she realized a speeding ticket would have been less damaging than his defensive reaction.

All of us have these emotional hot spots and they are usually related to our self-worth, self-esteem, or self-image. Our particular hot spots are largely determined by our past emotional experience, especially the relationship with our parents and others in early childhood. We may not know what these hot spots are until our spouse triggers them by their comments. There is almost no way to avoid these defensive experiences. What we can do is learn from them, something we must do or these defensive episodes will forever be barriers to communication (we'll talk more about this in chap. 16). In this chapter, we are focusing on understanding defensiveness.

Unresolved Conflict

Unresolved conflict in a marriage can also be a source of defensiveness. If we have not resolved our differences, we feel somewhat estranged from each other and are therefore more vulnerable to being defensive. Some couples who fail to resolve conflicts over a period of years draw the conclusion that they are not compatible and, in fact, are enemies. Their rationale becomes "an enemy is out to get me; therefore, I must always be on my guard." They basically begin looking for something to which they can respond defensively. Subconsciously, they are expecting attacks from time to time, and they live in a state of readiness to defend themselves.

Unresolved conflict does not mean that these couples never discuss conflicts. Periodically, they may have long and heated discussions about conflicts. The problem is they never reach a solution. After the heat has intensified to a certain point, they drop the conversation and withdraw from each other, leaving the conflict unresolved. Then when the spouse says something that is emotionally tied to this unresolved conflict, the person will have another defensive response.

Sometimes the situation is heightened by a feeling of guilt on the part of one or both of the spouses. This is particularly true when an individual knows that something they are doing or not doing is wrong, but they are unwilling to change their behavior. Their guilt predisposes them to be defensive when the spouse mentions a subject related to their guilt.

After several months or years of unresolved conflicts, we begin to hear inner voices that say: "I know I married the wrong person." "How could I have let myself get into such a mess?" "I can't believe that my mate is so inconsistent." The unresolved conflicts lead us to think that we are incompatible and that our spouse is not really on our side; therefore, we expect him or her to put us down. So, we must be ready to fight back. The more we give such messages to ourselves, the more we come to believe them and the more hopeless we feel. Such self-talk pushes one away from the marriage.

I am not suggesting that we should not talk to ourselves—all of us do. I am suggesting that in our self-talk we should seek to talk about specific events and issues rather than allowing the unresolved conflicts to push us toward making broad generalizations about our spouse and our marriage. The road to marital growth is always one step at a time. We are better if we focus on seeking to resolve one conflict rather than living under the burden of many unresolved conflicts.

Physical Deprivation

A third source of defensiveness is physical deprivation. We are more likely to be defensive when we are deprived of sleep, exercise, or proper diet. Many also have observed that when they have suffered a severe illness, they are often more defensive. This is rooted in the changes that have taken place in the body and perhaps depressed feelings over one's physical condition.

We may also be defensive with our spouse when things are not going well in other areas of life, such as unusual stress on the job, at church, with the children, or with aging parents. Any of these stressors can heighten our likelihood of being defensive.

We can take positive steps to correct these situations. Nothing substitutes for proper sleep, exercise, and diet. Looking for ways to lower our stress level and taking positive actions will make us less defensive.

Typical Defensive Reactions

When a person experiences defensive emotions, the reaction is typically expressed in one of three ways.

Verbal Retaliation

The most common way of expressing defensive feelings is *verbal retaliation*—lashing back at the person who stimulated our defensiveness. Keep in mind that defensive responses involve two things: protecting something and opposing something. Usually we are protecting our self-worth, and we are opposing anything and anyone who threatens us in this area. Thus, the statements we make in verbal retaliation will almost always fit into one of these two categories.

Let's say that a husband and wife have agreed that he will be responsible for the yard work—mowing grass, trimming shrubs, raking leaves, and so on. One afternoon, he arrives home and discovers that the shrubs around the front porch have been trimmed. His temperature rises before he opens the front door. His first statement to her is, "So you just couldn't wait until I did the shrubs, huh? Why do you always put so much pressure on me? Why does everything have to be done on your timetable? I suppose the next thing you will be doing is mowing the grass!" He walks out of the room, and she wonders if the golden rule— "Do unto others as you would have them do unto you"—is still true. She was trying to help him, but what she got for her effort was verbal retaliation.

Notice the two elements of protection and opposition. He is seeking to protect his own self-esteem. He feels good about himself when he provides for his family and keeps the yard looking nice. In his mind, his wife's behavior makes him a failure, or at least communicates that she views him as a failure. His little emotional soldiers jumped to attention to protect his self-esteem. Note also his opposition to his wife when he accuses her of taking further steps in the future to dehumanize him when he suggests that, next, she will "mow the grass." His verbal retaliation may succeed in keeping her from violating his territory again, but it has also deeply hurt her, placing a wedge between the two of them. Verbal retaliation almost always has a detrimental effect on relationships. It shuts down communication between the couple. Though the argument may be brief and the matter not mentioned again, an emotional wedge remains in the relationship.

Scripture speaks of the folly of such verbal retaliation. Paul admonishes us, "Do not repay anyone evil for evil" (Rom. 12:17). Thus, even if we feel that our spouse's behavior is designed to do us harm (which is usually not the case), we are still challenged not to respond in a negative way. Paul further admonishes, "Do not avenge yourselves" (Rom. 12:19). The writer of Proverbs says, "A fool gives full vent to his anger, but a wise man holds it in check" (Prov. 29:11). In Proverbs 20:3 we read, "Any fool can get himself into a quarrel." Both Scripture and experience indicate that verbal retaliation is destructive to marital unity.

Withdrawal

A second response to defensive emotions is *withdrawal*. In this reaction, emotional defensives are disturbed, but for whatever reason, the person does not verbally retaliate. He simply walks away from the situation, perhaps mumbling to himself but never fully expressing his feelings to his spouse. He walks into his private world and practices what professionals call "internal dialogue"; that is, he talks to himself verbally and/or mentally. He relives the situation—perhaps many times—each time feeling the hurt and the anger toward his spouse. Fuming inside, he keeps his distance from his mate geographically and emotionally.

Some Christians feel that withdrawal as a defensive reaction is preferred over verbal retaliation. The fact is that it may be just as detrimental to the relationship. Withdrawal and silence about one's inner feelings leads to defensive self-talk. Also, emotions that are repressed will likely show up in other areas of life, sometimes even in physical symptoms such as headaches, backaches, nausea, and stomach disorders. Withdrawal allows no opportunity for processing the defensive emotions, thus no opportunity to learn from the experience.

Scripture also condemns silent suffering. In Matthew 18:15, Jesus instructed, "If your brother sins against you, go and rebuke him in private. If he listens to you, you have won your brother." Certainly this principle applies to marriage. Therefore, if you feel that you have been wronged, it is your responsibility to share your perceptions with your spouse in a positive way and not to suffer in silence. In Ephesians 4:31 we are instructed, "All bitterness, anger and wrath, insult and slander must be removed from you, along with all wickedness." Thus, withdrawal and silent suffering are not the biblical answers to our defensive emotions.

Speaking through Children

For couples who have children, there is a third way of responding to defensive emotions: *speaking through the children.* We verbalize our emotions to a child rather than to the spouse. "Do you know what your mother did?" is the beginning of a release of defensive emotions. Jake's mother used her children to get what she wanted from his dad. Jake deeply resented his mother's manipulation, but he felt sorry for her and usually took her side. As a result, he and his dad were emotionally distant from each other. Later, when Jake became an adult and got married, he was very uncomfortable when his wife wanted him to handle a problem between her and the children or when the children came to him with a problem between themselves and their mother. Jake learned from experience that speaking through children is not a positive way to handle defensive emotions.

This may well be the most destructive response of the three in that it involves not only the husband and wife but also an innocent child. Scripture warns against gossips "saying things they shouldn't" (1 Tim. 5:13). To prejudice a child's mind against one of his parents because of the adult's own defensive reaction is extremely unfair. The emotional objective of such behavior is to build oneself up by tearing down one's spouse. The truth is, everyone is hurt by such behavior. It is unfair to the spouse, and it is destructive to the child caught in the middle, hurt and confused.

ða ða ða

It should be obvious that speaking through children, withdrawal and silent suffering, and verbal retaliation are not biblical answers to our defensive emotions. Still, most of us can identify with one or all of these reactions. Defensiveness is a subjective reaction designed to defend ourselves from emotional pain by opposing the person or thing that threatens us. We cannot eliminate defensive reactions, but we can learn to direct them to positive ends. In chapter 16 we will talk about how to make the most of defensive reactions.

CHAPTER SIXTEEN

OVERCOMING THE BARRIERS OF DEFENSIVENESS

D efensive reactions often stifle communication and erode intimacy. As one wife said, "I was looking forward to a nice romantic evening with my husband until he looked up from the table where he was balancing the checkbook and said, 'If you don't stop spending so much money, we're going to have to file bankruptcy.' I became livid. Then all my thoughts about a nice romantic evening flew right out the window. We spent the next thirty minutes arguing, and then I stalked off to the bedroom and cried myself to sleep."

All of us experience emotional defensiveness, but it need not be destructive. In fact, defensiveness can lead to more meaningful communication and deeper intimacy. This chapter is devoted to helping you learn how.

Getting to the Root of the Problem

Let's begin by trying to understand the roots of defensiveness. Plants do not exist without roots, nor do defensive reactions.

Virtually all defensiveness is rooted in our emotions. Behind the defensive behavior is an emotional history.

Sometimes, these emotions are easy to identify, making our defensiveness easy to understand. For example, in the illustration above, the wife felt condemned, controlled, and angry at her husband's comment about her spending patterns. Her defensiveness had roots growing in several directions. For starters, she knew that last week he had purchased a set of golf clubs for five hundred dollars. Thus, she thought that his comments about her spending were hypocritical and unfair. Besides this, for the past six months, as her husband balanced the checkbook each month, he asked her why she had made certain purchases. Since she contributed as much to the family income as he did, she perceived this as an effort on his part to control her. Another root easily identified upon reflection was that during her college years her father often berated her about her spending. She and her father did not have a very loving relationship. Now she saw her husband becoming her father. This wife did not have to look far to see why she responded defensively.

On the other hand, some emotions are deeply buried, and defensiveness seems to be out of proportion to the issue. Trivial issues mask deeper, more troublesome ones, often issues left over from, or rooted in, childhood and now surfacing in the marital relationship. Phil and Marilyn agreed that she would work outside the home and he would help her in household responsibilities. She would continue as chief cook and he as assistant because both agreed that he did not have the basic culinary skills to maintain life. Three months later, he is standing in the kitchen asking, "What can I do?" when Marilyn snorts, "I don't care what you do—just get out of here. I'll do it myself."

"I just wanted to help you," he said.

"I know, but you are more trouble than you are worth," she replied. "I would rather do it myself." Silently, Phil turns and walks out of the kitchen—and out of intimacy with Marilyn. The inner voices start talking, and he feels hurt and confused.

After a great deal of reflection, Marilyn discovered that she felt guilty about not being a good mother to her two preschoolers. Her own mother was a full-time homemaker when Marilyn was young, and she always thought that she would do that when she had children. Phil, however, had pressed for the bigger house, which forced her to work outside the home. When they had discussed it, she had agreed, but inwardly she resented it, and she resented him for pressing for the house. She also recognized feelings of estrangement from him. His presence in the kitchen reminded her of this emotional distance. As he stood in the kitchen like a child asking how he could help, she reasoned, "If he were a man, he'd be out there making enough money so that I could fulfill my responsibility as a mother and wife." Unfortunately, she never expressed these thoughts to Phil.

Without any knowledge about Marilyn's emotions, Phil was clueless as to why she ordered him out of the kitchen. His hurt was heightened by his own history. His mother always told him that he had better get a wife who could cook or he would starve to death. Once she had tried to teach him how to make a pie, but when he burned the crust, she yelled him out of the kitchen. The message was clear: he did not meet his mother's expectations. He also felt that he did not rate highly in his father's eyes. His dad had warned him against majoring in music in college, arguing that he would never be able to support a family by playing a trumpet. Phil was strong-willed, so he pursued music anyway. Now his wife, whose acceptance he so deeply desired, told him to get out of the kitchen. He felt reduced to the unacceptable child again—except now as an adult, it hurts even more deeply.

Three weeks later after the kitchen incident, Marilyn cannot understand why Phil is so withdrawn and seemingly uninterested in her. It certainly cannot be because of her request for him to get out of the kitchen, she reasons. And she is right. Neither of them knows why because he buried his emotions and never let her know they existed. Neither of them will ever understand their defensive reactions until they first identify and then share with each other the emotional roots of such defensive behavior.

Many couples never get to the root of the problem. All of their discussion centers on the comment made in the kitchen. Usually they condemn each other for getting upset over such a simple statement. Then they dismiss the whole matter as being caused by the stress they are both under at work. After a few weeks of silence, they start talking again and go on until the next episode. Understanding the emotional roots of our defensive behavior is essential if we are to overcome this barrier to communication.

Discovering the emotional roots of our defensiveness is not super difficult, but it does require conscious reflection. Withdraw from the situation and ask yourself, "Why did I get so defensive about that?" Take a sheet of paper and list the answers that come to mind. Your immediate responses will likely focus on the surface issues. Marilyn's first response was, "I'm defensive because he's in my way; he's no help. He just makes my job more difficult." Upon further reflection, however, she realized that her defensiveness had nothing to do with her husband's culinary skills but was rooted in her self–esteem, which was tied to her ideas of being a good mother. Sometimes the roots of our defensiveness are buried in emotional patterns that are quite removed from the surface issues.

Another question that helps uncover the roots of defensiveness is, "What happened in my childhood or adolescence that may be related to my present defensive reactions?" If your defensive reaction is extremely strong, it is almost always rooted in childhood or adolescent experiences. Rachel was a rather mild-mannered woman, but three months after marriage, her husband Brad blew his nose while sitting at the dinner table. Rachel went ballistic. "What are you doing?" she said. "I can't believe you did that." Getting up from the table, she ran out of the house, got in the car, and drove away, leaving Brad sitting at the table flabbergasted. Later, as they sat in the counseling office, Rachel said, "I don't know why, but that annoys me more than anything. It's so uncouth."

Later in our session I asked Rachel the question, "Is there anything in your childhood or adolescence that is related to your defensive response?" She said, "I remember once, when I was about ten years of age, my grandmother had come for a visit. She was the most wonderful person in my life. She was so good to me. I admired her greatly. One evening when we were having dinner, I had a cold and I blew my nose on my napkin. My mother got angry and dismissed me from the meal, sending me to my room. I was humiliated. What would my grandmother think of me now? I felt I had destroyed her confidence in me. I knew she would never want to have a meal with me again. It was the worst night of my life."

Rachel discovered the roots of why her defensive reaction was so strong when her husband, Brad, blew his nose at the dinner table. In her mind that was about the worst offense he could commit. She had not consciously thought about it, but when Brad blew his nose at the table, strong emotions from the past surfaced. Upon reflection, she was able to relate her past experience to her present defensive behavior.

Emotional roots to defensive behavior can be discovered by almost any individual who is willing to spend some time reflecting upon his/her history. Most individuals will not need psychotherapy in order to discover these roots. It is worth the time and effort because understanding the emotional roots of our defensive behavior is essential if we are to overcome this barrier to communication.

Learning from Our Defensiveness

Defensive emotions are not sinful although our verbal responses and behavior can be. Nonetheless, it is always harmful to ignore such defensive emotions. They are like those little red lights on the dashboard of our cars. They call for our attention, seeking to inform us of something that needs to be serviced. We ignore them to our peril. There is much to be learned about ourselves from our defensive feelings, and there is potential growth in the marital relationship when a couple deals honestly with their defensive reactions.

In Romans 8:28 we read, "We know that all things work together for the good of those who love God: those who are called according to His purpose." *All things* must include defensive emotions. It is God's intention to use every experience in life for our good. The ultimate good that God has in mind is to make us like Christ (see Rom. 8:29). Therefore, we should make every effort to cooperate with God in seeking to gain good from these experiences.

First, what can I learn about myself from my defensive reaction? I suggest you begin by focusing on the event itself, answering the following questions:

- *What emotions did I feel when I responded defensively?* Hurt? Anger? Disappointment? Shame?
- *What message did my spouse's statement communicate to me?* That I am inadequate? That I am stupid? That I am a child? That I don't mean much to him/her? That my ideas are unimportant?
- *What did my response, verbally or behaviorally, communicate to my spouse?* That they are stupid? That they are not going to control me? That I greatly dislike what they did? That I will not tolerate it in the future? That I don't like them?
- *What did my response reveal about me?* This is where your reflection upon the roots of your defensiveness will be helpful. Your defensive reaction may reveal something about your history that you have long forgotten. It may reveal an expectation you brought into the marriage but have never shared with your spouse.

Another approach to learning is to focus on the larger aspects of your marriage that may be related to your defensive behavior. The following questions may be helpful:

- What attitudes do I have toward my spouse that may explain my defensive behavior?
- Do I see my spouse as inferior intellectually?
- Do I see my spouse as passive or aggressive or controlling?
- Do I sense that my spouse has failed me in some way?
- Do I feel loved and appreciated by my mate?
- If I could ask my spouse to change a behavior or verbal message, what would I ask?
- What other aspects of my marriage may have influenced my defensive response?

Answering these questions will help you begin to learn something from your defensive reaction, whereas ignoring the issue simply sets you up to repeat it again later.

Discussing the Issues

After you have spent time reflecting upon your defensive behavior and learning what you can about yourself and your reactions, it is time to call for a "level 5" discussion with your spouse. In chapter 7 we examined five levels of communication. Level 5 was "Let's be honest." On this level your objective is to be honest but not condemning, open but not demanding—allowing one another to think and feel differently, and trying to understand why your spouse feels and thinks the way he does. You seek to understand and look for ways to grow together. Hopefully your spouse will agree to participate in a level 5 discussion. The most important ingredient is that both of you focus on listening to the other person. Look at him when he talks, and try to hear what he says. Nod your head to encourage him to continue. Tell him what you understand him to be saying, and let him clarify. Make it your goal to understand his feelings and why he feels the way he does. You may want to pray the prayer of St. Francis: "May I seek to understand rather than to be understood." If both of you seek to understand, you will be understood.

You might request such a conversation by saying, "I realize that last night I got rather defensive when . . . . I really want to learn from that experience. I spent an hour this afternoon reflecting on the experience, trying to learn something about myself. I think I have some insights, and I would like to share them with you and get your feedback. Is this a good time to talk?" If it is not a good time, then try to set a time in the future to have your talk.

When you begin your level 5 conversation, remember to speak for yourself by using "I" statements. "I really appreciate you giving me this time. I realize that my reaction to your behavior last night was very defensive. I think I understand myself better upon reflection, and I'd like to share with you some of what I think was going on inside of me when I responded the way I did. Let me say first of all that I'm not pleased with the words I said to you or with my behavior. I want to learn better ways to express myself when I get defensive, but I also hope that you will try to understand me so that we can continue growing together." Then, as clearly as you can, express the insights about yourself that you gained as you reflected upon the experience. Share with him/her the experiences in childhood that you think are tied to the current incident and the manner in which you found his/her behavior to threaten your self-identity.

If you are on the receiving end of a conversation initiated by your spouse to address his/her defensive reaction, remember that your major responsibility is to listen sympathetically. Keep eye contact with your spouse while he/she is talking. Let your body language say, "I am listening. I care." Don't interrupt; don't change the subject. Let your spouse talk and explain as clearly as they can what was happening when they reacted so defensively. Rephrase what you hear them saying, and make sure that you understand what they mean. After listening, you might say, "Do you mean . . . ?" and then rephrase as completely as possible what you think your spouse is saying. Let your spouse continue until they finally say, "Yes. That is what I mean." Now you have the whole picture and will likely understand what has been going on inside your spouse. Be open to the insights your spouse is sharing. In the New Testament, Peter instructed husbands to live with their wives "with understanding" (1 Pet. 3:7). The writer of Proverbs observed, "A fool does not delight in understanding, but only wants to show off his opinions" (Prov. 18:2).

Paul admonished us to "accept one another, just as the Messiah also accepted you, to the glory of God" (Rom. 15:7). A husband and a wife who accept and understand each other indeed bring praise to God. Such conversation also brings much positive fruit emotionally. If you feel that your spouse understands your needs, you will likely feel loved, and intimacy is enhanced. On the other hand, the feeling that we are misunderstood keeps us at arm's length.

Exploring Change

Now that each of you better understands the defensive behavior, it is time to explore ways of relating to each other in a more constructive way. As you discover each other's emotional hot spots and realize that these are related to your spouse's self-esteem, you will be motivated to find new ways of expressing yourself or new ways of behavior that will not threaten your spouse's self-esteem. If you are the one experiencing the defensive behavior, you may now suggest to your spouse what you think would help in future similar situations. The purpose is to learn how to share ideas without stimulating defensiveness in your spouse.

You might say, "When you start your sentences with 'You should' or 'You ought,' I feel like you are acting like my father or God and that I am your child. Intellectually, I know that's not what you are doing, but emotionally, that is what I feel. So perhaps in the future if you want me to do something, you can say, 'In my opinion . . .' or 'I think it would be helpful to me if you would . . . .' I don't think I would get defensive if you are simply sharing it as your opinion or are giving me information."

Another important principle in diffusing defensiveness is to learn to make requests rather than demands. A statement like the following will likely stimulate defensive feelings: "If you don't clean those gutters soon, they are going to fall off the house. They already have trees growing out of them." Your spouse is less likely to become defensive if you make a more positive request: "Do you think it would be possible for you to clean the gutters this weekend?" One is a request; the other is a demand. Demands are far more likely to stimulate defensive reactions on the part of your spouse.

When we experience our spouse's acceptance as we talk about our emotions and the reasons we respond the way we do, we create an emotional atmosphere for greater intimacy. Do not condemn yourself or your spouse for having defensive emotional responses, but seek to learn something from each such experience by discussing them openly and lovingly. If you do, you will find that they begin to occur less and less frequently. You are learning to build each other's self-esteem by accepting each other's feelings and trying to learn new ways of relating to each other. The more deeply you feel that your spouse is with you, that he believes in you, that he values you, the less defensive you will be.

🕊 🕊 🕊

As we affirm our own worth and the worth of our partner, we are obeying one of the two greatest commandments: "Love your neighbor as yourself" (Mark 12:31). God intends for us to love in order to build each other up, not to tear each other down with thoughtless words or a critical spirit. Feeling defensive is not a sin, but defensive reactions can be sinful. We must value ourselves and the marriage relationship enough to pay attention to our feelings. We must not allow defensiveness to become a barrier to communication and intimacy. In chapter 17, we visit the Garden of Eden in an effort to explore the communication and intimacy patterns of Adam and Eve before sin entered the world.

CHAPTER SEVENTEEN

INTIMACY:
NAKED AND UNASHAMED

In an effort to understand marital intimacy, I invite you to
return with me to the Garden of Eden. The biblical account
in the Book of Genesis is brief but extremely revealing. Before
Eve arrived, Adam had a place to live (2:8–9), a vocation (2:15,
19–20), a clear statement of rules (2:16–17), and open fellowship
with God. In today's harried society, many men would visualize
this as heaven. In the mind of God, however, something was
missing.

What Adam Lacked

Whether or not Adam knew it, he had not yet experienced
one dimension of life. Perhaps God was creating a felt need in
Adam when he gave him the assignment of naming "all the beasts
of the field and all the birds of the air" (2:19). As Adam observed
the male and female genders of each animal, perhaps he became
keenly aware that he had no counterpart. All of the animal world
seemed to exist in pairs, but he was alone.

God's answer to Adam's aloneness was the creation of Eve and the institution of marriage. When Adam saw Eve, he exclaimed, "This is now bone of my bones and flesh of my flesh; she shall be called 'woman,' for she was taken out of man" (2:23). It was his spontaneous response when he first laid eyes on Eve. Awakened from a deep sleep, he beheld the work of God and knew that she was for him. Adam's analysis is revealing. He saw in her his counterpart, taken out of him but separate from him. This simple, graphic picture of creation is at the heart of what marital intimacy is all about.

Intimacy is not sameness. Becoming close does not mean we become identical, that we lose our individuality, that our lives are blended into some new whole and we lose our personhood. On the contrary, it is our uniqueness, our separateness, that makes intimacy possible. If we were identical, there would be nothing to discover, no new thing to experience, no joy of exploration. Because we are different, there is the potential for exploration and discovery, and the excitement of the process adds a whole new dimension to marriage. Two people entering into each others' lives, discovering and being discovered—that is intimacy!

Something deep within Adam responded to something deep within Eve. This was no superficial encounter. This was the heart of humanity responding to another human heart, another who was closer to him than all else in the universe. She was formed differently from him, not from the dust but from his own rib.

Adam called her woman not man. Had he called her man, she would have been a duplicate. Instead, he called her woman because she was "taken out of man." Related? Yes, but different, unique, complementary, the counterpart of man, one to whom man could relate, one who could understand and be understood, one who could communicate on the same level, one who would also have fellowship with God, one who is highly intelligent, one also made in God's image and, thus, the only one of God's creatures able to relate to man in such an intimate fashion.

One of the essential ingredients of intimacy is allowing each partner to be himself/herself. Intimacy must never be interpreted as the effort to conform the spouse to your ideals, to your thinking. To reduce another to being a duplicate is not the purpose of intimacy. In intimacy we are trying to grow close together—not destroy the "otherness" but to enjoy it. Men and women are different, and we must not, even with good intentions, seek to destroy those differences.

The other half of Adam's statement focused on kinship or relatedness. When he said, "This is now bone of my bones and flesh of my flesh," Adam was expressing his sense of kinship with this woman. She was different from all the animals whom he had named, radically and totally different. She was related to him; she was not "the long-lost friend." Rather, she was the much longed for friend whom he had not known before. She was the answer to his inner desires for companionship, for someone to whom he could relate as an equal.

Some may question whether the biblical account of the woman being created from the rib of Adam would indicate that she is inferior to man. However, the idea of inferiority is found nowhere in the biblical text. Rather, how she was created is a declaration of the capacity for intimacy. The fact that God chose to make Eve from the rib of man is another indication of God's wisdom and his intention for deep intimacy in marriage. If God had made the woman from "the dust of the ground" as he had made man, she may have looked the same as Eve, but there would not have been the physical, emotional, and spiritual ties with Adam. God's creative act planted deep within the male and female a natural desire for each other—a kinship, a relationship, a potential for extraordinary closeness. Nothing in this biblical account indicates inferiority; rather, the emphasis is on intimacy.

It is because of these two realities—similarities and differences—that man is motivated to "leave his father and mother and be united to his wife" (2:24). Because woman was taken from man, she is related to man. There is something deep within the man that cries out for the woman and something within the woman that longs for the companionship of the man. We were made for each other. To deny our similarities is to deny our basic humanity. We were formed by the same God, from the same fabric, for the purpose of relating to each other. On the other hand, to acknowledge our similarities and deny our differences is a futile effort to refute reality. Our theme is not competition; our theme is cooperation. We were made not to compete but to complement. Adam found in Eve a resting place, a home, a relative—one who was deeply and uniquely related to him. And Eve found the same in Adam.

Marital Paradise

What was life like for this first man and first woman? We are left largely to our imagination, but one brief word is given: "The man and his wife were both naked, and they felt no shame" (2:25). The old saying "One picture is worth a thousand words" must surely apply here. Do you see the picture? Male and female? Naked? Without shame? It is the most graphic picture of marital intimacy. Two distinct persons; equal in value; with bone-deep emotional, spiritual, physical relatedness; totally transparent; without fear of being known. It is that kind of openness, acceptance, trust, and excitement to which we allude when we use the word *intimacy*.

The emphasis is on transparency and openness, the freedom to know and to be known. Obviously the primary reference in this verse is to physical nakedness, but implied is also emotional, spiritual, and intellectual nakedness. The picture is that of transparency, of being known totally by another. As fallen, self-centered creatures, we often rebel against being known. To be known opens the possibility of being condemned and rejected. We fear that if our mate really knew us, he/she would not like us; therefore, because of our fallenness, it is almost impossible for us to imagine being totally known by another person. We have been trained well to put "our best foot forward" by sharing only those things that we feel will enhance us in the eyes of others, all the while covering our self-centered and sinful actions and thoughts. Such an attitude developed as a self-preservation technique in a sinful world, but it limits the level of intimacy one may experience with his/her spouse. Even as Christians, we may never regain the paradise of total intimacy, but to turn away from the potential of high-level intimacy is to consciously turn away from God's original pattern.

One can only imagine the conversations Adam and Eve shared. Did Adam tell her all that had transpired before she arrived? Did he introduce her to the animals by name? Did he speak of his care for the garden before she came? How much of each day did they spend in each other's physical presence, and how much time did they spend apart? We are not told, but we can only imagine that when they were together, conversations were revealing. Nothing was held back, for they had no fear of being known. They had nothing to be ashamed of.

It is hard to read the biblical account without experiencing an emotional longing for a return to paradise. This longing motivates us to seek and find that special man or that one-of-a-kind woman with whom we can share our lives. Our desire for an intimate relationship leads us to make deep, all-encompassing vows to each other when we marry.

Modern Eden

Does anything in contemporary life parallel the pristine excitement of Eden when Adam and Eve first related to each other? I want to suggest that it is the experience we commonly call "falling in love." It is an emotional, spiritual experience fully as spontaneous as that moment when Adam first saw Eve and she, him. The experience of falling in love is not of human making. It is totally beyond us. It happens to Christians and non-Christians. It has the same elements of that initial meeting of Adam and Eve:

- Feeling a sense of amazement
- Feeling a sense of belonging to each other
- Knowing that we were meant for each other
- Feeling something within each of us that cries out for something deep within the other
- Sensing that God arranged our meeting

- Experiencing a willingness to be open with each other, to share our deepest secrets, and to know in our hearts that we will love each other no matter what
- Having a willingness to give ourselves totally to each other

In present-day society—which associates falling in love predominantly with sex, lust, and exploitation—we sometimes lose the vision of true love. But in all true love there lies a germ of self-sacrifice and self-giving. I am talking about that kind of love. As the Scriptures say, "There is no fear in love; instead, perfect love drives out fear" (1 John 4:18). We are not afraid to reveal ourselves because we have the inner assurance that we will be accepted no matter what we share. Whereas in the early stages of a dating relationship we may conceal much about ourselves, once we are truly "in love," there is a taste of nakedness. This kind of love gives us the courage to make deep, all-encompassing commitments at the marriage altar. Would a man or woman without love ever make such comprehensive vows?

Can you go back to those early days when you first experienced the sensation of love for your spouse? Do you remember the promises you made in those days? "I'll go anywhere with you." "Nothing you could tell me would ever cause me to stop loving you." "Whatever is best for you is what I want as long as I live." Perhaps you should read some love letters you wrote in those early days to help you remember the kind of self-sacrificing statements you made. You likely expressed a deep sense that you belonged to each other, that your togetherness was destined by God. "I can be open and honest with you." Nothing short of this kind of conviction would lead a man or a woman to take seriously the commitment of marriage.

Though we cannot actually reinstate the transparency of Eden, in a love relationship we see reflected the image of the original. As in the rest of life, the image of God is marred by the fall of man, but his image is not destroyed. In many ways, we still reflect the hand of our Creator.

Sadly enough, this taste of transparency is far too brief for many couples. As one husband said, "I don't know what happened after we got married. Before marriage, she was so loving, exciting, and caring. After marriage, she became demanding and critical." His wife's response? "Before marriage, he was so thoughtful. I was the focus of his life. After marriage, it was as though I didn't matter anymore. Everything else was more important. How can he change so radically?"

Many couples echo the sentiments of this couple. Indeed, the same was eventually true of Adam and Eve.

಼ ಼ ಼

Sometimes it is helpful to revisit the days of courtship when the two of you were madly "in love." You may want to write a paragraph or two about your emotions and behavior in those days. How did you view your spouse then? How does that compare with the way you see him or her now? What were your dreams of the future then? If your dreams did not quite come true, what happened? This brings us to chapter 18, in which we focus on the sad reality of "Paradise lost."

CHAPTER EIGHTEEN

THEN CAME CLOTHES

The picture of open transparency in Eden's garden was soon marred. Eve was still "bone of his bone and flesh of his flesh," but she was no longer naked, nor was he. Fig-leaf aprons covered their physical bodies. This act of concealment also affected their emotional, intellectual, and spiritual relationship. Their transparency of thoughts and emotions no longer existed. The same was true in their relationship with God. They hid in the bushes when God came to visit because they now had something they did not wish God to know about them. They were ashamed to face God, for they were guilty of violating his trust. It is this violation of trust that always causes us to conceal ourselves from God and from each other. When we seek to do what is right and abide by the teachings of Scripture, we desire open fellowship with God. When we consciously violate the teachings of Scripture and disregard the commandments of God, however, we are much happier to stay away from church and anything else that reminds us of God.

Why do so many contemporary couples have so little intimacy ten or fifteen years after the marriage commitment? In their early days together, they spent hours together, talking and listening. Seldom a week passed that they didn't make discoveries together—taking a hike, going on a picnic, or simply sitting in the clover together.

What happened to the sense of discovery, the sense of openness, of wanting to be close to each other? Very likely, it is the same thing that happened in the Garden of Eden. Their personal sin has created within them a spirit of fear, distrust, or guilt. They now have something to be ashamed of, something to hide. They cannot afford to be open because openness will lead to judgment. So they protect themselves, withdraw, stay away from each other. No longer do they sense their similarities, but their differences. No longer do they sense the "bone of my bones and flesh of my flesh," but their separateness. They can hardly believe that they had once been close. They have replaced love with selfishness.

The same thing that happened in the Garden has happened to us. Eve replaced her love for Adam with her own selfish desires for what she saw. Adam replaced love for God with his own selfish desires. Love always looks out for the interest of the other person; selfishness places me at the center of the universe, and my desires as more important than anything else. When selfishness replaces love, our behavior and our words render us guilty, ashamed, and fearful to be transparent with our spouse. We know that to be transparent is to be found out, and to be found out is to be judged and condemned.

It usually starts with little things. He wants to go to the gym and work out: she wants him to go shopping with her for some new towels. He goes to the gym anyway, and a block is erected in a wall between them. He wants sex; she chooses to watch the late night movie. Another block is added to the wall. Many couples have allowed this process of self-centered living to grow through the years until they actually conceal most of their thoughts and emotions. The part they reveal to each other is only a tip of the iceberg. The majority of their thoughts and feelings are concealed beneath the surface. As one husband said, "If I told her how I really feel, she would probably leave me." Or, as a wife said, "I'm afraid to tell him what I really think because I fear his anger." Obviously, these couples experience little marital intimacy.

Our insecurities (our sense of shame) push us to clothe ourselves lest we be known and rejected. We want to avoid being hurt. We desire to keep things as comfortable as we can; therefore, we do not share anything that we feel may be objectionable to our spouse. Some of us have layered ourselves with emotional clothes. Our spouse has little idea who we really are. Our thoughts, desires, frustrations, and feelings are all buried beneath many protective layers. We have been hurt and we hurt; we have been violated and we have violated. Many couples have failed to deal with these violations. Their answer has been to put on another layer of withdrawal and to hide from their spouse.

Let's go back to the Garden of Eden. How long were Adam and Eve naked? Until the day they sinned. The Scriptures say, "They realized they were naked; so they sewed fig leaves together and made covering for themselves" (3:7). They hid themselves from God, and when God asked Adam why he was hiding, Adam answered, "I heard you in the garden, and I was afraid because I was naked; so I hid" (3:10). Now they had reason for shame. With this experience of fear, no longer could man and woman tolerate nakedness. The guilt was too intense; the shame, unbearable. They turned away from each other and from God. Intimacy was marred.

The first thing Adam did was to blame Eve (3:12), and she in turn blamed the serpent (v. 13). Before the day was over, God announced the consequences of their sin, made them garments of skin for covering, and directed them out of the Garden. I have often wondered what Adam and Eve said to each other when God left them at the end of the day. Paradise became a memory and pain, a reality—for Eve, increased pain in child bearing; for Adam, increased pain in tilling the soil. For both, intimacy now required effort. In order to be close and experience the excitement of oneness, they had to go through the painful experience of confession and forgiveness. Without these two, their fears and their shame would keep them apart.

The Scriptures share very little of Adam and Eve's relationship after their sin. We know that they had sex, for they had sons and daughters (5:4), but we do not know the level of openness or the depth of their oneness. We can wonder if Adam often mentioned Eve's sin to her, if he ever truly forgave her, and she, him. How long did it take to rebuild trust? Was their relationship with God fully restored? If so, then perhaps their marriage was fully restored. We can only guess about that.

What we can learn from their experience is that no husband and wife will experience high-level intimacy unless they are also experiencing oneness with God. The broken relationship with God is the reason for fear and shame as we stand face to face with each other. If we can face God, knowing that we have confessed our sins and have been forgiven, then we have the potential of facing our mates with the same openness. Keeping our integrity with God is essential to experiencing genuine intimacy in a marriage relationship.

Having reestablished a climate for intimacy by means of confession and forgiveness, we continue to regain paradise by means of open, loving communication. Our past failures remind us of our potential for hurting each other, but we must not allow past failure to keep us from seeking God's ideal of marital intimacy. Daily we pray that God will fill our hearts with love for our spouse. We open ourselves to being God's channel for expressing love. We seek to be honest about our fears. In expressing our fears to our spouse, we hope to gain assurance, encouragement, and support. Since we are fallen creatures, we recognize that we have the potential to fail each other, to walk away from love, and to revert to selfish living. The goal of intimacy is not obtained by denying our failures but by acknowledging them immediately and asking forgiveness. This willingness to deal with our failure keeps the potential for intimacy alive. When we fail to deal with our sins against each other, we literally destroy the possibility of intimacy.

The road back to intimacy is the road back to love. It begins with a willingness to confess our self-centered living and to ask for mercy and forgiveness—first of God and then of our spouse. It is followed by the decision to ask God to pour his love into our hearts (see Rom. 5:5) and to let us be his agents for loving our spouse. It is a return to the one thing that drew us together in the first place—genuine love. For those who recognize that their marriage was originally based on selfishness rather than true love, it is the discovery of true love that leads them to true intimacy.

God alone can give this kind of love, and he has promised it to all who ask. He has told us that we are responsible for loving each other (Eph. 5:25; Titus 2:3–4). God has never commanded us to do anything he will not give us the power to do. Love is a choice. It is an attitude, a way of thinking, and a way of behaving toward our spouse. When we choose to walk the road of love, God will give us the power to experience it. When we love on the heels of confession and forgiveness, we will again experience a climate in which intimacy can blossom, in which we can be open and not condemning, in which we can be forgiving and accepting, in which we have the sense again that we belong to each other.

I am not suggesting that because of God's forgiveness we are transported back into the Garden of Eden. That was not true for Adam and Eve, nor is it true for us. I am saying that because of Christ we have a restored relationship with God. We once again can relate to him as our Father, and he to us as his children. The openness, freedom, and joy of his presence can be ours. We are still fallen creatures, prone to sin. However, because of his love he reaches out to us and offers forgiveness and power to live as "renewed" people. It is this restored fellowship with God and the vision of future complete redemption in Christ that makes life not only bearable but enjoyable.

Our marriages will never attain the transparent openness between Adam and Eve before the fall. Yet, because of Christ and the reality of forgiveness, we can experience a measure of intimacy unknown by non-Christians. We focus on this biblical ideal because we believe this is the direction in which God is leading us. The apostle Paul teaches us that "all things work together for the good of those who love God"; that is, to make us like Christ (Rom. 8:28–29). It is this ideal of Christlikeness that is our goal.

In like manner, it is the ideal of God's original marriage pattern that we hold before us and to which we aspire. It gives us hope and vision as to what marriage can become. Some may ask, as did Megan, "Can I ever trust him again? Before, I trusted him so completely, but now my trust has been destroyed. I don't know if I can ever trust him again." The answer to Megan's question is yes. Trust is based on the belief that I am loved, that my spouse has my best interest in mind. Trust is destroyed when the spouse's behavior indicates that my belief is untrue. In fact, the spouse has chosen to walk his own way rather than love me. His behavior has thus destroyed my trust.

The loss of trust is an inevitable result when one spouse fails to live up to his/her covenant; that is, when one of us acts in a self-centered way rather than a loving way. When it becomes obvious by my behavior that I am putting my own interest above the interest of my wife, I have abandoned my pledge to love. My wife will inevitably lose trust in my words and promises in the future. That trust cannot be restored with simple promises to do better. It is only as my behavior indicates that I have truly repented and, in fact, love her that trust will find rebirth.

Trust can be regained by reversing the process—first with confession of failure and the willingness to forgive. Then we take the pathway of loving behavior. In word and deed, we give evidence that we seek what is best for our spouse. Such a pathway of loving actions over a period of time will lead to the rebirth of trust.

Trust is like a fragile plant. Whenever it is destroyed, it resembles the plant's being broken off at the ground. In time and with loving care, trust can grow and blossom again. A growing sense of trust in each other is a part of creating a climate in which intimacy can be experienced.

When a couple recognizes more distance than intimacy in their relationship, more separateness than togetherness, more selfishness than love, and thus more aloneness than unity, they are at a crossroad. A decision must be made: continue the road of separateness and aloneness, or regain the ground that has been lost and perhaps conquer ground that was never theirs.

We call this decision *commitment*. It is an act of the will in which two persons decide to walk together and then, with the help of God, take the necessary steps to grow toward intimacy. It takes time to make these steps. Steps of confession, forgiveness, love, and trust are not taken in a moment. But with one step at a time, any couple can rebuild intimacy in their marriage relationship.

The Scriptures teach the reality of forgiveness and real change when a person confesses sin and asks for God's help in the future. Thus, the Christian has grounds for hope that the non-Christian does not have. If God, who is holy, can forgive us for our offenses against him, then we, who are not holy, can forgive each other for our trespasses. If God, who made us in the beginning with freedom of choice because of his love for us, continues to affirm our freedom, surely he will give us the power to do right when we choose to do so.

Our past failures are covered, not by clothes of our own making, but by the clothes that God has made. The Scriptures call this *the robe of Christ's righteousness*. As God made clothes of skin for Adam and Eve, thus slaying the animals, Christ—who was slain for our sins—now provides us an adequate covering. Therefore, we can come into God's presence without shame. It is this same reality of forgiveness between a husband and wife that allows us to again be open with each other and experience the joy of knowing and being known.

இ. இ. இ.

Our relationship with God is central in building an intimate marriage. Adam and Eve were separated from each other after they separated themselves from God, and the same will be true for us. Reestablishing a relationship with God by confessing sin and accepting his forgiveness gives us the divine help we need to regain or establish intimacy in our marriages. In the next four chapters we will focus on emotional, intellectual, sexual, and spiritual intimacy.

CHAPTER NINETEEN

EMOTIONAL INTIMACY

It was a cold afternoon in February. Emily was the last of my appointments. She had called earlier in the day, insisting that she see me today. Without any of the polite formalities of greeting, she sat down and simply blurted out, "I don't know how to say this. But I just don't feel connected to Greg anymore. I don't know what he is feeling because he never talks to me, and I don't like what I'm feeling. At one time I thought we had a good marriage, but then Greg's job and the babies pulled us in two different directions. It's like we're two strangers living in the same house. I don't know if Greg loves me. He never tells me, and he certainly doesn't act like it. I don't know if I love him anymore, and that really scares me."

Emily's plea for help illustrates the importance of emotional intimacy in a marriage. Without it, husbands and wives become roommates or business partners. The heart of the marriage is diseased.

What is emotional intimacy? It is that deep sense of being connected to another. It is feeling loved, respected, and appreciated while at the same time seeking to reciprocate. Emotional intimacy is feeling secure and excited about our lives together. It is positive regard for each other because we feel that our hearts beat together.

How does a couple maintain or regain such intimacy? I believe it begins with the choice to seek to meet each other's emotional needs. What are these emotional needs that seem to be so vital in producing a successful marriage? Perhaps the three most basic are the need to feel loved, to feel respected, and to feel appreciated. To feel loved is to have the sense that my spouse genuinely cares about my well-being. Respect has to do with feeling that my spouse has positive regard for my personhood, intellect, abilities, and personality. Appreciation is that inner sense that my spouse values my contribution to our relationship. When a husband and wife feel loved, respected, and appreciated by each other, they are experiencing emotional intimacy.

Handling Negative Emotions

Some couples make the mistake of believing that simply sharing emotions with each other will produce emotional intimacy. The fallacy of this idea is easily demonstrated. When Ryan says to his wife Stephanie, "I feel hurt, disappointed, angry, and betrayed," he is honestly sharing his feelings, but he obviously does not have emotional intimacy with her. Still, sharing such emotions may be the first step in paving the road to emotional intimacy. Apparently, Stephanie's behavior or his perception of her behavior has stimulated these emotions inside of him. His willingness to share his emotions gives her valuable information to which she can have an honest response. If she says, "I'm sorry. I regret my behavior. I wish I could go back and undo it, but I know I can't. With God's help, it will never happen again. I hope that you can forgive me," she is removing rubble so they can continue down the pathway of intimacy.

On the other hand, she may respond, "Honey, I don't know who told you that, but it's not true. I did not do that. I beg you to check your sources because I assure you that it is not true. If it were true, I could understand why you would feel hurt, disappointed, angry, and betrayed. But believe me, it is not true." Ryan now has an opportunity to check his sources and establish the truth. His emotions will follow suit depending on what he finds. If he realizes that he was wrong, he may return to say, "I'm sorry that I chose to believe the worst about you. That was unfair of me. I'm so glad it's not true. I hope you will forgive me for jumping to the wrong conclusion." Such an encounter illustrates the importance of sharing emotions as the first step toward building emotional intimacy.

If Ryan had held his emotions inside and never expressed to Stephanie that he was feeling hurt, disappointed, angry, and betrayed, these emotions would have stood as blockades to emotional intimacy. It is only in sharing our negative feelings that we have an opportunity to process them and move beyond them.

From time to time, all of us have negative feelings toward our spouse. Almost without exception, these feelings are stimulated by the behavior of our spouse. She promised to take his shirts to the laundry and failed to do so. He promised to mop the kitchen on Saturday. It's now 11:30 P.M. and the floor is still dirty. He had hoped that she would recognize his birthday. She didn't. She had expected a word of appreciation for trimming the shrubs, but if he noticed, he never told her.

How do we share these negative emotions in a positive way? I suggest saying to your spouse, "If I had a negative emotion, is this a good time to share it?" This informs your spouse that something is going on inside of you. It also gives them an opportunity to get emotionally prepared to hear what is troubling you. If this is not an appropriate time from their perspective, you then set a time to share your negative emotions.

My wife and I know that occasionally each of us will have negative feelings toward the other, so we covenant that when we feel negative, we will share our feelings with each other with a view toward resolving the issues that originally stimulated the emotions. Couples who regularly share and work through such emotions are building emotional intimacy. Those couples who internalize these emotions will typically find themselves withdrawing, arguing, or being critical of their spouse, none of which builds emotional intimacy.

Meeting Emotional Needs

When we deal positively with our negative emotions, processing them openly with our spouse, we clear the air. The smog is gone, and we are free to reach out and seek to meet each other's emotional needs: the need for love, the need for respect, and the need for appreciation.

Love

How then do we meet each other's emotional need for love? I have written extensively about the five fundamental languages of love.[1] Let me briefly recap them. The first love language is Words of Affirmation—using words to affirm your spouse. "You look nice in that dress." "I really appreciate your cleaning out the garage." "Thanks for taking out the garbage." "The song you sang in church was beautiful. You did a great job this morning." The ancient Hebrew proverb says, "Life and death are in the power of the tongue" (Prov. 18:21). Mark Twain once said, "I can go two months on a sincere compliment." Most of our spouses need more than that. I suggest a compliment a day.

The second love language is Giving Gifts. My academic background is anthropology. I have studied cultures around the world but have never discovered a culture where gift giving is not an expression of love. A gift means, "He was thinking about me. Look what he got for me." The gift need not be expensive. Haven't we always said, "It's the thought that counts"? But I remind you, it is not the thought left in your head that counts. It is the gift that came out of the thought in your head. A flower, picked out of your neighbor's yard, may do wonders for your spouse. (Be sure and ask your neighbor before picking.)

A third love language is Acts of Service—doing something that you know your spouse would like for you to do: cooking a meal, washing dishes, vacuuming floors, washing the car, mowing grass, trimming shrubs, changing the baby, getting white spots off the mirror, anything that you know your spouse desires. When your spouse makes a request, they are giving you a clue as to what would make them feel loved. "Honey, do you think you could clean the gutters out this weekend?" is not a nag but a request for love.

The fourth love language is Quality Time—giving your spouse your undivided attention. Taking a walk in the neighborhood, going out to eat, looking at each other and talking, sitting on the couch with the TV off, talking to each other, taking an afternoon to hike a mountain trail, or sitting together on a mall bench can speak deeply to your spouse. You care enough to give your time. When you give your spouse twenty minutes of undivided attention, you have given him/her twenty minutes of your life. It is a powerful emotional communicator.

The fifth love language is Physical Touch. We have long known the emotional power of physical touch. Holding hands, embracing, kissing, sexual intercourse, your arm around her shoulder, your hand upon his leg as you drive down the road all communicate emotional love.

Out of the five love languages, each individual has a primary love language. One language speaks more deeply emotionally than the other four. Seldom do a husband and wife have the same love language. By nature, we speak our own language; that is, whatever makes us feel loved, that's what we do for our spouse. But if that is not his/her primary love language, it will not mean to them what it would mean to us emotionally. The key to meeting your spouse's emotional need for love is learning to speak his/her primary love language.

A husband may be mowing the grass, washing the car, blowing leaves, and vacuuming floors to show his love to his wife, but if her love language is Quality Time, her love tank may still be empty. He will wonder how a woman could feel unloved if her husband does all of these things for her. The problem is not his sincerity; the problem is he is speaking the wrong love language.

The wife who gives her husband affirming words but seldom touches him affectionately may think that she is expressing love. But if his primary love language is physical touch, his love tank will be empty regardless of her sincerity.

Learning to speak your spouse's love language will not necessarily be easy. The person who grew up in a home where affirming words were seldom heard may find it difficult to verbalize such words to his/her spouse. But if we want to have emotional intimacy, we must learn to speak our spouse's primary love language. When the husband and wife are speaking each other's love language consistently, they are well on the road to emotional intimacy. The need to feel loved is perhaps our most basic emotional need. When this need is genuinely met, we have taken a giant step toward emotional intimacy.

Respect

Because we are made in the image of God, we are creatures of great value: male and female. Something deep within us affirms that we are creatures of respect and dignity, that God's imprint is upon us. Consequently, when our spouse's words or behavior demean us, we feel violated. There can be no emotional intimacy between a husband and wife without respect. Respect begins with an attitude: "I acknowledge that you are a creature of extreme worth. God has endowed you with certain abilities, insights, and spiritual gifts. Therefore, I respect you as a person. I will not desecrate your worth by making critical remarks about your intellect, your judgment, or your logic. I will seek to understand you and grant you the freedom to think differently from the way I think and to experience emotions that I may not experience."

Such an attitude paves the way for you to show respect for your mate. Respect does not indicate that you agree with your spouse on everything. It does mean that you give them the freedom to be an individual. No two humans are alike in the way they think and feel. Respect says, "That's an interesting way to look at it," not "That's the dumbest thing I've ever heard." Through the years, I have been amazed at how inhumane spouses often treat one another. I remember one husband who said to his wife, "I can't believe that you are a college graduate and think so illogically." Then there was the wife who said, "If you had a brain the size of a pea, you could figure out why I am so upset." Such degrading statements create animosity not intimacy.

If you are going to communicate respect to your spouse, you must choose to treat him/her as a human. All humans are people of dignity and worthy of respect. All humans are unique because they are created by a God who is supremely creative. Allowing your spouse to be the person God created him/her to be is the first step toward communicating respect. Trying to argue your spouse into compliance with your views shows disrespect for his/her personhood.

To show respect is to look for the God-given giftedness of your spouse and to affirm and encourage their uniqueness. "I would never have looked at it that way. It's very helpful to get your perspective" is a statement of respect. "I don't see how you could look at it that way. Anyone would know that is wrong" is a statement of disrespect. We can disagree with our spouse without being disrespectful. Respect gives people the freedom to be who they are, to think what they think, and to feel what they feel. A wife does not expect her husband to agree with her all the time, but neither does she expect him to call her ideas stupid. A husband knows he is not always right, but he doesn't want to be called a liar.

Respect says, "Honey, I don't agree with you, but I know there must be some good reasons why you see it that way. When you have time, I would like to hear more of your thoughts on that." Respect says, "Honey, I'm sorry you feel hurt. That was certainly not my intention. Let's talk about it."

Disrespect often grows out of emotional insecurity. If I am insecure in who I am, I may put you or your ideas down in order to elevate myself. Yet when I am secure in my own personhood, realizing that I am a child of God and of infinite value, then I am free to allow you to be who you are.

One wife raised the question, "How can you respect your husband when you know his lifestyle violates the teachings of Scripture?" My response is, "You do not respect his lifestyle, but you respect his freedom to choose that lifestyle." God made us creatures of choice realizing that we would sometimes make unwise decisions. He does not remove our freedom even when we make choices contrary to his Word. However, he does hold us accountable, allowing us to suffer the consequences of our poor decisions. Thus, a wife shows respect when she says to her husband, "It hurts me to see you go against the teachings of Scripture. I know you will suffer the consequences of your choices, and that hurts me deeply because I love you so much. But I want you to know that I respect your right to make your own decisions." She is speaking the truth with love and respect.

Appreciation

The third element of emotional intimacy is the sense of being appreciated. When we express appreciation, it means that we recognize the value of our spouse's contribution to our relationship. Each of us expends our energy and abilities each day in ways that benefit our relationship. To sense that our spouse recognizes our efforts and appreciates them builds emotional intimacy between the two of us. Thus, appreciation may focus on our observation of the things our spouse has done today: "It feels so clean in here. I really appreciate your hard work today." "I think this meatloaf is the best I ever tasted. I really appreciate your work in preparing this meal." "Honey, I don't always tell you this, but I want you to know that I really appreciate the fact that you make up the bed every morning." "I don't tell you this every week, but I want you to know that I always appreciate the fact that you mow the grass every weekend. Some of my friends complain that their husbands will wait three weeks. You always mow it regularly, and I deeply appreciate you and your hard work."

On the other hand, appreciation may focus not on our spouse's performance but on their abilities: "I love to hear you sing. You are so gifted." "God has given you the gift of teaching. I marvel at your ability to lead our class in meaningful discussion." "I really appreciate the fact that you are so good in keeping our books. You know that is not my strong suit, and I really appreciate the abilities you have in that area and the way you keep our finances straight." "I want you to know that I don't take for granted all the repair jobs you do around the house. You save us thousands of dollars every year because you are able to do so many things. I am fortunate to be married to you." Or, "I am so thankful for your ability to provide for us. I know that when something goes wrong, I can pick up the phone and call the plumber or the repair man knowing that there will be enough money in the checking account to pay for it. I don't take that for granted. I really appreciate your ability and your work in providing for us financially."

Appreciation may also focus on our spouse's personality: "I am so thankful for your positive spirit about things. Some of my friends say that their spouses are always down, always seeing the negative, and they are depressing to be around. It's not true for me. Your spirit is always positive. No matter what happens, you see something good in it. I want you to know that I really appreciate that about you." "When we go on vacation, I am so thankful that you are a planner. If it depended on me, you know that we probably wouldn't have a place to stay half the nights. But the way you plan our vacations, it is so fun and relaxing because you have taken care of all the details. I want you to know I really appreciate that." "You know if it weren't for you. I would live a boring life. I really appreciate your spontaneity. You have pulled me into so many fun things that I would never have done on my own. It's so much fun living with you."

Everyone wants to feel appreciated, and even in the worst of spouses there is always something you can appreciate. I remember the lady who said about her alcoholic husband who never held a steady job for more than six months, "He's a wonderful whistler." Expressing appreciation for the positive things you see in your spouse is a strong motivator for him/her to pursue the things that elicit appreciation. Don't wait until your spouse is "better." Begin where you are. Express appreciation and watch your spouse flourish.

ãã ãã ãã

In this chapter we have looked at the positive ingredients in building emotional intimacy: love, respect, and appreciation. We have also talked about the necessity of sharing and processing with each other our negative emotions lest they become roadblocks to emotional intimacy. As we move to chapter 20, we will discuss intellectual intimacy.

CHAPTER TWENTY

INTELLECTUAL INTIMACY

In the fabric of life our thoughts and feelings are woven together in an inseparable fashion. However, I have chosen to treat them separately for the purpose of understanding and gaining insights into developing these parallel lines of intimacy. When I speak of intellectual intimacy, I am talking about that sense of closeness that develops between a couple who has learned to share their thoughts freely with each other. It is developing an understanding of each other by entering into each other's world of thought. Intellectual intimacy is the sense of being included into the other person's world rather than shut out.

The thoughts we share may be profound and have global significance or they may be as personal as sharing one's desire for an ice cream cone. The thoughts may be attached to decisions or simply shared as information. Obviously, the nature and significance of our thoughts will have a great deal to do with our spouse's emotional response to the thoughts. For example, the shared thought of buying a $50,000 boat may solicit quite a different response than sharing the thought of buying a hamburger. Nonetheless, intellectual intimacy is that freedom to share thoughts with each other, confident that we will be heard and will receive an honest and caring response from our spouse.

We all know the story of the wife who worked to put her husband through college or graduate school. She spent most of her energy working and being a mother while he grew intellectually. Shortly after he got his degree, the marriage broke up. This scenario happens too often to be mere chance. In many cases, part of the answer lies in the fact that the couple did not share life intellectually. Because the husband was living in a totally different world from his wife's, they grew apart. That's why some colleges and graduate schools make provision for spouses to attend lectures and workshops without being enrolled. If they keep abreast in certain areas, intellectual communication with their spouse is enhanced.

Then there is the situation where a wife embarks on a new career that she finds exciting and intellectually challenging. Her husband has little interest in her career, so she soon stops talking about any of the things she finds interesting at work. As they grow apart, the husband blames the wife's job for their separation. In reality, the culprit was a lack of intellectual intimacy.

Living in different worlds for several hours a day does not necessarily lead us apart. The problem is the lack of intellectual communication—sharing our thoughts, our interests, our experiences with each other, and listening with interest. A husband in a highly technical field of work once said to me, "We have been married for sixteen years. At this juncture in our marriage, I cannot carry on an intelligent conversation with my wife because our worlds are so far removed from each other. She has no understanding of the things I live with every day and apparently little interest." His statement illustrates the result of a lack of intellectual intimacy.

A husband and wife do not need to be totally conversant in all the technicalities of each other's work or interests. However, they should learn enough to be able to communicate and gain a sense of togetherness. A visit to each other's workplace is often a positive step toward enhancing communication and intellectual intimacy.

On the other hand, intellectual intimacy does not necessarily focus on our vocations. It results from sharing our thoughts, experiences, and desires openly with each other. Couples who learn to do this in an open and responsive context will discover that conversation can be extremely exciting. However, trying to share such information in a negative, emotionally charged atmosphere may be virtually impossible. That is why developing emotional intimacy (which we discussed in chap. 19) is so important.

The Art of Listening

Much of our silence in marriage can be attributed to uncertainty as to how our spouse will respond to what we share. Thus, good listening creates a climate for open talking. One husband who had tried sharing "three things that happened to me today and how I feel about them" (which we discussed in an earlier chapter) said after some weeks of trying, "I really don't get the sense that my wife is interested when I am sharing things that happen to me throughout the day." His perception of disinterest may be rooted in himself and his own insecurity, but it may also be rooted in the listening patterns his wife has developed.

Most of us are more interested in sharing our ideas than in hearing the other person's ideas. It takes two good listeners to make one intimate marriage. Research has shown that in troubled marriages, a high level of misunderstanding exists between the spouses when they talk. Such misunderstanding is often rooted in poor listening.

If I feel misunderstood, I may feel rejected. If I feel rejected, I will likely talk less in the future. Most of us could profit from sober reflection on Proverbs 18:2: "A fool does not delight in understanding, but only wants to show off his opinions."

Intellectual intimacy requires that we share our ideas, but it is fully as important that we listen to our spouse's ideas. Hearing, understanding, and accepting our spouse's ideas, even if we don't agree, is foundational to creating intellectual intimacy. None of us freely shares our ideas if those ideas are always opposed and condemned.

Many people have never learned how to accept an idea with which they do not agree. In their minds, accepting an idea is giving approval to it. Acceptance and approval, however, are quite different. Acceptance means giving the person the freedom to think the way he thinks. Approval means agreeing with his conclusions. We can always accept our spouse's ideas though there may be times when we don't agree with them.

Approval is expressed in such statements as: "I agree." "Let's do it." "That's a wonderful idea." "That's a loving thought." "That's a brilliant concept." Acceptance, on the other hand, is expressed by such statements as: "That's an interesting thought. I'm not sure I agree, but it is worth exploring." "Is that really the way you think about that? I am quite surprised. I had no idea that was the way you were thinking." "I don't think I could ever agree with that idea, but if that is what you really think, we will have to try to find an answer to our differences because I respect your freedom to think differently than I." Such statements do not cloak our disagreement, but neither do they condemn the other person's ideas. The purpose of listening is not to pass judgment but to hear what the other person is thinking, to become aware of her ideas, to enter the world of her thoughts. You can evaluate those thoughts later if such evaluation is requested, but intellectual intimacy requires only that we listen attentively for the purpose of understanding the other person's ideas.

Another skill in the art of listening is to give your mate your undivided attention when he/she is talking. Some time ago I visited two people by appointment on the same afternoon. As I talked to the individual in the first office, he continued to open mail, make notes to himself, and shuffle books on the desk. He seldom looked at me. I quickly got the feeling that he was not interested in our conversation. When I entered the office of the next person, he turned off his computer, laid a book on top of his manuscript, turned and faced me, and looked at me as we talked. He gave the impression that nothing could be more important than our conversation. Intellectual communication and intimacy are enhanced when we give each other our undivided attention when we talk.

Some individuals pride themselves on being able to watch TV, listen to the radio, read a book, and carry on a conversation with their spouse all at the same time. Although some individuals can do this (I am not questioning their ability), I am suggesting that to build intellectual intimacy such multifaced listening is not an asset. If my spouse gets the sense that I am not interested in what she is saying because my attention is given to other things, then she may lose interest in continuing to share her thoughts. Undivided attention communicates love and concern for the other person. To create the best possible climate for intellectual intimacy, our actions need to communicate to our spouse that nothing is more important than hearing what he/she has to say.

There are times when we cannot give each other undivided attention. The best way to constructively handle these situations is to simply tell the truth. The husband says to his wife, "Honey, I left the water running in the tub. Let me turn it off so I can give you my undivided attention." An avid basketball fan may say to his/her spouse, "The next two minutes are the most crucial. Let me finish this so I can give you my undivided attention. I really want to hear what you have to say and make sure I understand it." Most individuals will respond positively to such honest statements. On the other hand, when one spouse continues to stare at the basketball game on television, making no verbal explanation as his/her spouse is talking, it will likely stimulate negative emotions and a negative response in the mind of the one trying to share. The husband who dashes up the stairs toward the tub without telling his wife what he is doing will likely communicate to her that what she has to say is unimportant.

"Stop, look, and listen" is a good motto when your spouse is talking. You can also enhance communication by using nonverbal messages that indicate your undivided attention. Such things as nodding your head, pulling your chair closer, turning off the television, reaching out and touching them as they speak, and other gestures can communicate your interest in what your spouse is saying.

Good listening requires thoughtful concentration. Focus on trying to understand the message your spouse is communicating. Words often have different meanings to different people. Therefore, you must ask questions to clarify the meaning. Many of our misunderstandings come because we assumed that we understood what our spouse meant when, in fact, we missed the whole point.

Recently my wife and I were leading a marriage enrichment retreat. As I headed for the shower on Saturday morning, she said, "Honey, hang my skirt on the back of the door." When I saw the skirt hanging from the shower curtain rod, I assumed that was the skirt to which she was referring and that she didn't want me to get it wet as I took a shower. So I took the skirt outside the bathroom and hung it with her other clothes. Thirty minutes later, she walked into the bathroom and said, "You missed the whole point." "Point about what?" I asked. She said, "I asked you to hang the skirt on the back of the door." "Yes, and I did," I responded. "No," she said. "You hung it with the rest of the clothes. I wanted it on the back of the door in the bathroom so the steam would take care of the wrinkles." "Oh," I said. "I did miss the whole point. I'm sorry." It was a simple thing and no irreparable damage was done to our marriage, but if I had practiced the principle of active listening, I would have clarified what she meant rather than assume that I understood.

Clarifying questions should never be designed to push your spouse into an intellectual corner by questioning the validity of their statements. You simply want to make sure that you understand their ideas. A husband says, "I'm not sure I am going to get this project finished by Friday." The wife responds, "You mean you are afraid you are not going to have time to get it done by Friday?" to which the husband responds, "Well, it's not a matter of time. I don't think I have the information I need and I'm not sure where to find it." "So lack of information is the problem?" the wife asked. "Well, that and I'm just not sure I really want to do this. I get tired of putting together reports that are never read," he says. "So you feel that a lot of what you are asked to do on the job is a waste of time?" Now, they are into a conversation about his job satisfaction and the possibility of changing jobs.

How different the conversation would have been had she responded to his initial statement of "I'm not sure I am going to get this project finished by Friday" by saying, "Oh, you've got plenty of time. I'm sure you'll get it done." Such a statement would likely have ended the conversation, and she would never have known his thoughts and feelings related to his job. Clarifying questions can become annoying if asked too often, but they often lead to engaging conversations that build intellectual intimacy.

Creating a Climate for Intellectual Communication

Every individual is unique. What helps one person may be a detriment to another. Discussing how you talk and listen to each other may help you discover new patterns of communicating. Your spouse may find it annoying when you continue to explore his meaning by asking questions similar to the ones discussed above. On the other hand, he may welcome such exploring. Your wife may be seeking a supportive statement from you after she shares an idea. She may be encouraged to talk more if you make such statements as "I understand." "I certainly agree with you on that." "Yes." "I see." Then again, she may find such statements patronizing and annoying.

Your spouse may want you to evaluate his ideas, to share your opinions. Or the opposite could be true; such an evaluation may cause him to stop talking almost immediately. When you say such things as "I don't agree with that" or "I think that is a bad idea," you may stop the flow of information from your spouse or get into an argument. An open conversation in which the two of you discuss what makes it easier or more difficult to talk to each other could be extremely helpful.

What response on the part of your spouse would make it easier for you to continue talking when you are trying to share an idea? For example, do you want him to nod, to look at your eyes as you speak, to lean forward in the chair—or do these things annoy you? When you are sharing an idea and your husband realizes that he disagrees with your idea, how would you like for him to express his disagreement? In what way could he share his disagreement without coming across in a condemning manner? Would it be helpful if he started by saying, "I want you to know that I give you the perfect freedom to believe that. At the same time, I want to share with you my own point of view"? Or, would you want him to say, "That idea is extremely interesting, and you may be right. But, let me give you another perspective"? Share with your spouse what would make intellectual communication easier for you.

Couples who have little understanding of what helps communication flow are likely to do and say things that stifle communication. Often, these undiscovered but unhealthy patterns of communication have been barriers for years. If we discover and remove these barriers, we will enhance intellectual intimacy.

One wife said, "Every time I share an idea with my husband, he always pounces on it like a dog on a rabbit, tearing my idea to shreds. I come away feeling like a total failure in his eyes. I have become very reluctant to share my ideas." It is possible that this husband has very little understanding of what his conversational patterns do to his wife and how detrimental they are to intellectual intimacy.

If a husband says, "I really feel worried about where we are going to get the money for Meredith's college," and his wife's response is, "Christians shouldn't worry. Why would you worry? You know that God is going to take care of it," as she reaches for the Bible to read him a verse. It will likely be a long time before he shares his thoughts and anxieties with her again. He was not looking for a sermon but for understanding and emotional support. He wanted her to know what was going on inside his mind. He needed to be accepted as he was at the moment. Her fast answer gave him the sense that she understood little of his dilemma. She treated lightly something that to him was extremely serious. Learning to identify these negative patterns of communication and to change them will help deepen intellectual communication and intimacy.

Creating a safe place in which to talk is of utmost importance in developing intellectual intimacy. If we are afraid that our spouse will take personal information that we are sharing and use it against us, we tend to be reluctant to share. If we believe that they will disagree with our ideas no matter what they are, we become reluctant to share our ideas. "That's an interesting idea. I would like to hear more about that" fosters a climate of positive communication, whereas "Where did you get that idea? You know that's not biblical," stops the conversation or starts an argument. Intellectual intimacy evaporates. Creating a climate of security, where you know your spouse will receive what you are saying and not condemn your ideas, makes it easy for you to continue talking and will enhance intellectual intimacy.

ࡥ ࡥ ࡥ

I have chosen to discuss emotional and intellectual intimacy before sexual intimacy because the three are directly related. The level of emotional and intellectual intimacy will be a predictor of the quality of sexual intimacy. The couple who gives little attention to chapters 19 and 20 but still expects to make great strides toward sexual intimacy will likely be disappointed.

CHAPTER TWENTY-ONE

SEXUAL INTIMACY

God is the author of sex; therefore, sex is good. It is sometimes difficult to remember this in a society in which sex has been exploited. Sex is used as an advertising medium to sell everything from automobiles to toothpaste. Espionage movies picture sex as a weapon to get what one wants. Movies and daytime dramas picture sexual unfaithfulness as the norm and, of course, always highly pleasurable. Perhaps the greatest exploitation of all is the multimillion-dollar pornography business in which human sexuality is prostituted for financial gain. One could easily ask, "Does God really have an interest in sex?" It may seem that Satan is the author of sex and that it is one of his most effective tools. However, the opposite is true. God is the creator of sex; Satan is the distorter.

The Bible declares, "Marriage must be respected by all, and the marriage bed kept undefiled, because God will judge immoral people and adulterers" (Heb. 13:4). The word translated *bed* is the Greek word *koite,* from which we get our word *coitus* or "sexual intercourse." The message is clear. Marriage is an honorable relationship, and sexual intercourse within marriage is a beautiful experience. Outside of marriage, fornication (the normal biblical word for premarital sexual intercourse) and adultery (the biblical word for sexual intercourse with someone other than your spouse) are condemned.

What is this sexual act that Scripture portrays as such a beautiful experience within marriage but so strongly condemns outside marriage? If we understand the purposes of sexual intercourse, perhaps we will understand the prohibition against extramarital sexual relationships. Scripture declares, "God created man in his own image, in the image of God he created him; male and female he created them" (Gen. 1:27). Being a male or a female is not a modern innovation, nor is it the work of Satan. Sexuality is clearly labeled "made by God." Having made us sexual creatures, "God saw all that he had made, and it was very good" (Gen. 1:31). He who created sexuality and pronounced it good has revealed to us the purpose of sexual intercourse and the reasons he reserves it for marriage.

Purposes of Sexual Intercourse

The most obvious purpose of sexual intercourse within marriage is procreation or reproduction. In Genesis 1:28 God said to Adam and Eve, "Be fruitful and increase in number; fill the earth and subdue it." It has been said that this is the one command of God we have done a rather good job of fulfilling; we have filled the earth. In the Bible, children are always viewed as a blessing of God. For example, "Behold, children are a heritage from the LORD, the fruit of the womb is a reward. Like arrows in the hand of a warrior, so are the children of one's youth. Happy is the man who has his quiver full of them" (Ps. 127:3–5 NKJV).

In the ability to bear children, God has given us the opportunity to participate in creation. The act of intercourse has the potential of bringing together the egg from the female and the sperm from the male, thereby creating a totally new being. Most parents agree that few joys are greater than looking into the face of a newborn baby and knowing that he/she is a reflection of both mother and father. We have made an investment of ourselves in producing this child, and we tend to be committed to the child's well-being. This was God's way of providing a place of security for the rearing of children. A husband and a wife committed to each other for life provide the best possible setting for rearing children. Thus, God indicated that the sexual act that produces this child should be performed only in the context of marriage.

A second purpose of relating to each other sexually in marriage is companionship. We were not created to live in isolation. God himself said of Adam, "It is not good for the man to be alone" (Gen. 2:18). As we noted earlier, the Hebrew word for *alone* literally means "cut off; isolated." God's answer to Adam's aloneness was, "I will make a helper suitable for him" (Gen. 2:18). When God created Eve, he said, "They will become one flesh" (Gen. 2:24). Almost all commentators agree that the term *one flesh* has a primary reference to sexual intercourse. In the context of sexual union, we express our deepest sense of intimacy. The one flesh experience is more than a physical act. It involves our emotions, our spirit, our thoughts—the total person. The word *intercourse* itself communicates the idea of dialogue, of entering each other's life. No other human experience is more intimate than the sexual experience. It celebrates our emotional, intellectual, and spiritual intimacy. It is a bonding experience.

This physical oneness cannot be separated from intellectual, emotional, social, and spiritual oneness. It is the experience of intimacy in these areas that provides the setting for sexual intercourse to serve its highest purpose. It is the culmination, the celebration of the deep and intimate relationship we have with each other. Sexual intercourse itself will not create an intimate marriage although sexual intercourse will greatly enhance our sense of intimacy. It is both a celebration of intimacy and a means of deepening that intimacy.

The all-encompassing nature of sexual intercourse is illustrated by the apostle Paul, who says, "Do you not know that your bodies are members of Christ? So should I take the members of Christ and make them members of a prostitute? Absolutely not! Do you not know that anyone joined to a prostitute is one body with her? For it says, The two will become one flesh" (1 Cor. 6:15–16). Paul gave both a spiritual truth and a physical truth. In the spiritual realm, we are united with Christ in the deepest possible way so that we are one with Christ, a part of his body. On the human level, Paul spoke of the absolute absurdity of becoming one flesh with a prostitute, one with whom we have no relationship and no commitment. Because the sexual act is a bonding act, ultimately there is no such thing as casual sex. In the context of intercourse, something happens emotionally, socially, and spiritually, whether or not we desire it to happen. This is one of the reasons for the strong warning against sexual intercourse outside of marriage.

Lawsuits that sometimes develop after such a sexual encounter indicate the social nature of this experience. The emotional trauma of guilt, anger, resentment, loneliness, and so forth, that follows extramarital affairs indicates that our emotions were not turned off while we were involved in sexual intercourse. Sexually transmitted diseases stand as a reminder that sexual intercourse is a physical act. God's condemnation of extramarital sex indicates that it has a spiritual dimension. The fact that our minds relive the sexual experience, both the negative and positive aspects of it, long after the sexual act is over indicates that our intellect was active in the process. Thus, sexual intercourse involves the total person. It cannot be done simply as a physical act, giving only momentary release or pleasure.

A third purpose of relating to each other sexually in marriage is for pleasure. Some Christians have difficulty with the idea that God would have created sexual intercourse for our pleasure. These Christians think of God as looking over the banister of heaven saying, "Anyone down there having fun? Knock it off!" This, however, is not the biblical picture of God. The Bible pictures God as having done many things for our pleasure, and sexual intercourse is one of those. For example, in Deuteronomy 24:5, God laid down these instructions for Israel: "When a man has taken a new wife, he shall not go out to war or be charged with any business; he shall be free at home one year, and bring happiness to his wife whom he has taken" (NKJV). The words translated *bring happiness to* are Hebrew words that refer to the pleasure of relating to each other sexually. God said no war and no work; take a year to learn to pleasure your wife.

The Song of Solomon, found in the Old Testament, describes the pleasure related to sex in marriage. It is so passionate that some have even questioned why this book is in the Bible. We can only conclude that God wanted us to have a clear message about the pleasure he intended us to experience in relating to each other sexually. Listen to the words of King Solomon as he describes the pleasure of relating sexually to his wife:

How beautiful your sandaled feet, O prince's daughter!
Your graceful legs are like jewels, the work of a craftsman's
hands. Your navel is a rounded goblet that never lacks
blended wine. Your waist is a mound of wheat encircled by
lilies. Your breasts are like two fawns, twins of a gazelle.
Your neck is like an ivory tower. Your eyes are the pools of
Heshbon by the gate of Bath Rabbim. Your nose is like the
tower of Lebanon looking down toward Damascus. Your
head crowns you like Mount Carmel. Your hair is like royal
tapestry; the king is held captive by its tresses. How beautiful you are and how pleasing, O love, with your delights!
Your statute is like that of the palm, and your breasts like
clusters of fruit. I said, "I will climb the palm tree; I will
take hold of its fruit." May your breasts be like the clusters
of the vine, the fragrance of your breath like apples, and
your mouth like the best wine. [And she responds:] May
the wine go straight to my lover, flowing gently over lips
and teeth. I belong to my lover and his desire is for me.
(Song of Songs 7:1–10)

This was not a one-sided pleasurable experience. Listen to the wife's response.

My lover is radiant and ruddy, outstanding among ten
thousand. His head is purest gold; his hair is wavy and
black as a raven. His eyes are like doves by the water
streams, washed in milk, mounted like jewels. His cheeks
are like beds of spice yielding perfume. His lips are like
lilies dripping with myrrh. His arms are rods of gold set

with chrysolite. His body is like polished ivory decorated with sapphires. His legs are pillars of marble set on bases of pure gold. His appearance is like Lebanon, choice as its cedars. His mouth is sweetness itself; he is altogether lovely. This is my lover, this my friend, O daughters of Jerusalem. (Song of Songs 5:10–16)

We cannot deny that there is physical pleasure in sexual intercourse even without commitment. But it cannot be compared to the sexual experience within marriage. Notice the emotional, intellectual, and social implications of the wife's response in 7:10: "I belong to my lover, and his desire is for me." A deep sense of relationship and belonging is evident. Emotional, intellectual, and social dimensions enhance the sexual relationship. Without this larger dimension of commitment, we have violated the purpose of sexual intercourse and have cheapened it to merely a physical act.

Sexual Differences in Marriage

You may be thinking, *Enough of this idealistic, romantic picture of pleasure and companionship in sexual intercourse. Let's get to the real world. I have not found all of this to be true in my experience.* To be sure, mutual fulfillment in the sexual aspect of marriage is not automatic. It doesn't happen simply because we are married. I believe that is one reason why God instructed the Israelite newlyweds to take a year for a honeymoon. Just as we must grow together in intellectual and emotional intimacy through the years, we must also grow together sexually. If we simply do what comes naturally, we may never find mutual fulfillment in the sexual part of our marriage. Our sexual differences often become stumbling blocks to sexual oneness. Let's look at some of these differences.

Sexual Need

First, there is the difference in the nature of sexual need. The male's sexual need is physically based. Let's review the biology of the male sexual anatomy. The gonads are continually producing sperm cells, which are stored in the seminal vesicles along with seminal fluid. When the seminal vesicles are full, there is a physical push for release. In fact, there will be a release either through nocturnal emission, masturbation, or intercourse. This is the way God made the male.

For the female, the sexual need tends to be more rooted in her emotional nature, her desire to feel loved. If she feels love, she wants to be physically intimate with the husband who loves her. If there is no emotional intimacy, she may have little interest in sexual intimacy. Understanding and cooperating with this difference in the nature of our sexual need will deepen our sexual intimacy.

Sometimes we forget that the opposite sex is opposite. If husbands forget this, they can end up resenting their wives for not being like men, and vice versa. Men and women are not alike. The sooner we understand and accept our differences, the sooner we will be on the road to sexual fulfillment.

This difference also explains why many times the husband may desire to have sexual intercourse more often than the wife. Because his need tends to be physically based, he has a rather regular desire for sexual release whether or not things are totally right emotionally in the relationship. While the female's desire for sexual intercourse is tempered by her hormonal cycle, it is far more influenced by her emotional and intellectual relationship with her husband. The implications for a husband are that he must place much more emphasis on nonsexual love; that is, he must communicate his love and care for his wife in ways that are meaningful to her. He must learn to speak her primary love language regularly and sprinkle in the other four love languages. Without such emotional intimacy, he cannot expect her to be as responsive sexually as he may be.

Jeff has an argument with Vera in which he "loses his cool" and says some hurtful things to her. After thirty minutes of silence, while he watches television and she cries, they go to bed. He, trying to be kind and trying to make up for his harsh words, reaches out to touch her. She immediately withdraws, so he gets angry. He reasons, "I'm trying to make up for my failure," while she reasons, "You want sex. You don't love me at all. How could you be so cruel?" If Jeff understood the difference in the nature of the male–female sexual drive, he would give a verbal apology and assure Vera of his love. He would not expect sex until she has had time to recover emotionally.

Arousal Patterns

Another area in which we differ is in sexual arousal patterns. In spite of modern efforts to make us unisex, we continue to be male and female. The male tends to be sexually stimulated by sight to a far greater degree than the female. This difference explains why a husband can simply watch his wife getting undressed and be ready to have intercourse by the time she comes to bed. On the other hand, the wife may watch the husband undress and the thought of sexual intercourse never cross her mind. If a wife doesn't want to have sexual intercourse, I suggest she undress in the closet; if she wants to stimulate her husband, undressing in his presence is one way to do it.

The wife is far more stimulated by tender touch, kind words, acts of service, or quality time, depending on her love language. The implications of this difference for her husband are that he must not expect his wife to be as interested in sexual intercourse as he is when he has been stimulated by sight. He must take time and use kind words, tender touch, and other ways to help her feel loved in order to bring her to the same level of interest he has reached simply by sight stimulation.

One word of warning is necessary. Since the male is not very discriminating in the female objects that stimulate him, he may be stimulated by watching a female form on television or by an unknown female who walks down the sidewalk in front of him. Such stimulation is not sinful, but it may quickly turn to lust. In today's world where pornography is so commonplace, the Christian husband must be diligent in keeping his heart and mind focused on his wife. Lust is desiring what is not permitted. The following saying is attributed to Martin Luther: "We cannot keep a bird from flying over our head, but we can keep it from building a nest in our hair." Similarly, the Christian husband cannot keep all sexual thoughts from flashing across his mind, but he certainly must not feed these thoughts. The biblical challenge is to take every thought and emotion and bring it in obedience to Christ (2 Cor. 10:5). The husband is responsible for having "eyes only for his wife," and the wife who understands the nature of the husband's sexual arousal will understand the purpose of keeping herself attractive physically. The husband who understands this difference will give his wife assurance of his love and commitment so that her emotional need for security is met and she has no reason to fear his wandering eyes.

Sexual Response

Another difference is in the area of sexual response in the context of intercourse itself. The male's physical and emotional response tends to be fast and explosive whereas the female's response tends to be slow and lasting. One of the most common problems associated with this difference is premature ejaculation, when the husband reaches a climax very fast in the sexual experience and returns to a normal emotional state. The wife, who may be only in the beginning stages of sexual excitement, is left wondering, "What was supposed to be so special about this?" Understanding this difference in sexual response patterns will help us seek to cooperate with the way God has made us and find ways to meet each other's needs.

Many couples enter marriage with the idea that it is normal to have *simultaneous* climaxes or orgasms every time we have sexual intercourse. Because of the differences discussed above, most couples do not experience this, nor is it important in reaching sexual fulfillment. What is important is that each of us reaches a climax or orgasm if we so desire. Who reaches a climax first or the amount of time between the two climaxes is immaterial. Our objective is to meet each other's sexual needs. Many wives are content not to reach orgasm each time they have sexual intercourse. Because of fatigue or other reasons, she simply does not wish to expend the energy and effort necessary to reach climax. She is content to love and to be loved, to help her husband reach climax, and to be deeply aware of his love for her.

Each of us needs to know that our spouse is committed to our well-being and willing to "bring happiness to" us. If such pleasure is one-sided or if it is demanded of each other, we will never find mutual fulfillment. It is to be two-way, and it must be offered as a gift. We may *request* pleasures of each other, but we must never *demand* it.

People often ask, "Why did God make us with so many differences?" Why is it so difficult for us to find mutual fulfillment in the sexual part of marriage? Some have observed that the animals don't seem to have the same difficulties that humans have in this area. Animals simply "do what comes naturally." I believe that God gave us these differences because he intended sexual intercourse to be something more than a reproductive act. He intended it to be a deep expression of our love for each other. If we do not make it a loving experience in which each looks out for the interest of the other, we may never find mutual fulfillment. But if we make it a loving act, built on emotional, intellectual, and spiritual intimacy, then the physical act becomes a celebration and a further bonding of our lives with each other.

We have always had the right words. Haven't we said, "Let's make love"? In reality, however, we don't always make love; sometimes we just make sex. But when a husband has the attitude "How may I pleasure you?" and the wife has a reciprocal attitude, they will find the sexual part of the marriage to be mutually satisfying.

Creating Sexual Oneness

Sexual oneness means that both husband and wife are finding the sexual part of the marriage mutually satisfying. How can we obtain this goal?

Commitment

The foundation of sexual oneness begins with commitment. Couples who tend to use the threat of leaving each other as a club to get compliance are in effect destroying their marriage. Such statements as "Well then, I'll just leave" or "Why don't you get a divorce?" may be expressed as statements of frustration within the marriage, but such statements are like poison to sexual intimacy. Marriage is based on covenant not coercion. Covenant is, as we have studied earlier, a willing commitment. In the wedding ceremony we verbalized our commitment to each other: "For better or for worse, so long as we both shall live." This commitment must be regularly affirmed in both subtle and overt ways throughout the marriage. If each of us has the sense that our spouse is committed to us for life, that we need not fear desertion, then we have a climate for growing together sexually. Commitment creates a climate of security.

This commitment is not limited to simply staying in the marriage. It is a commitment to give ourselves to each other sexually. Nowhere is the biblical ideal stated more clearly than in 1 Corinthians 7:3–5: "A husband should fulfill his marital duty to his wife, and likewise a wife to her husband. A wife does not have authority over her own body, but her husband does. Equally, a husband does not have authority over his own body, but his wife does. Do not deprive one another—except when you agree, for a time, to devote yourselves to prayer. Then come together again; otherwise, Satan may tempt you because of your lack of self-control."

Our natural, God-given sexual desires are to be met within the marriage relationship. When this is done, we help alleviate the temptations that may come from outside the marriage. The challenge of 1 Corinthians 7:5 is that we will not cheat each other sexually. After we are married, we are to be committed to meeting each other's sexual needs. If we encounter problems in this process, we are committed to finding answers. If our emotional attitudes about sex have been marred or scarred from past experiences, then we are committed to finding healing so that we may grow in the joy of sexual intimacy. This kind of commitment creates a climate of security and hope.

Commitment says, "We will continue to grow together until both of us are finding mutual fulfillment in the sexual part of our marriage." Such commitment gives tremendous hope and creates a climate for growth. However, when one or both individuals expresses little interest in the other's sexual needs and makes little effort to learn or grow in this aspect of the marriage, a climate of hurt, disappointment, and, ultimately, hostility is created. In a Christian marriage such attitudes as selfishness must be recognized as sinful, and we must seek the forgiveness of God and our spouse as we give ourselves in fresh commitment to each other.

Communication

A second principle in deepening sexual fulfillment is: Communication supercedes performance. Much talk today emphasizes technique and performance as though these hold the key to sexual intimacy. This is a misplaced emphasis. Certainly the Scriptures do not condemn variety of posture and technique, but the biblical emphasis of intimacy is not on performance. Sexual intimacy is the result of a relationship, and relationship is fostered by communication. Sexual intercourse is not an act that establishes deep intimacy but one that presupposes it. Sexual problems will not be solved with mere techniques. Sexual foreplay begins not after we get in bed but twelve to sixteen hours *before* we get in bed.

If we do not keep the lines of communication open throughout the day—sharing in each other's lives intellectually, emotionally, and socially; by hearing and being heard, by understanding and being understood—we cannot expect sexual intimacy. The daily sharing time introduced earlier ("Tell me three things that happened in your life today and how you feel about them") is as important to sexual fulfillment as food is to the body. If we take time to hear each other, expressing interest in each other's experiences and feelings throughout the day, we create a climate in which sexual intimacy can flourish. All of the communication principles discussed in this book relate directly to obtaining sexual oneness.

We must exhibit a spirit of empathy and understanding. If the day has been filled with unresolved conflict, disrespect, and insensitivity, then it will be difficult, if not impossible, for us to find sexual fulfillment. From time to time someone says to me, "We just can't find time to talk with each other every day." My answer is that if we do not have time to talk, then we don't have time for sex. In essence, we don't have time for marriage. Wise couples make time to talk, and wise couples seek sexual fulfillment.

We must also communicate with each other about our sexual experience. Because we are different and because we have different desires and needs, we cannot expect to find mutual fulfillment if we do not openly discuss our needs. Thus, we must take time to share with each other what brings us pleasure in the sexual experience and what irritates us or discourages sexual excitement. These are to be shared not with a condemning attitude but with a view to sharing information that will be helpful in our efforts to bring pleasure to each other. "What one thing would you like me to do or not do that would enhance the sexual relationship for you?" This would be a good question for spouses to ask each other every three months for the next several years. Responding to the request of your spouse will strengthen sexual fulfillment.

When I suggest that communication supercedes performance, I am not minimizing the value of the many Christian books available that deal with common questions related to sexual performance. Most couples would profit from a discussion of such books.[1] What I am saying is that sexual fulfillment is not the result of discovering some "magical trick," but it is the natural result of building a loving relationship.

Love

A third principle that leads to sexual oneness is: Love is the garden where sexual intimacy grows. Love and sexual intimacy cannot be separated if we are to experience mutual sexual fulfillment. Because sexual intercourse involves not only the male and female sexual organs but also our minds, emotions, and spirits, the physical experience is greatly magnified by emotional, intellectual, and spiritual love. By *love,* I mean the conscious effort to look out for the other person's interest.

Love is both an attitude and an emotion. We choose our attitude, and this determines our emotions. If we choose to think the best of each other and look out for the other's interest, we will seek ways to express that attitude. As we express love in our spouse's primary love language, chances are the spouse will feel loved. We will also feel good about ourselves because we will know that we are making the right choice. Conversely, when we choose the attitude of apathy or hate—that is, choosing to "leave her alone" or "get even with him"—we will behave accordingly, and the spouse will likely feel rejected, unloved, or hated.

The individual who holds these attitudes will feel badly not only about his/her marriage but also about himself or herself.

The Christian husband and wife are challenged to express love unconditionally. God is our example: "But God proves His own love for us in that while we were still sinners Christ died for us!" (Rom. 5:8). We also read that "God's love has been poured out into our hearts through the Holy Spirit who was given to us" (Rom. 5:5). As Christians, we can express God's love to our spouses even when we do not have positive feelings for them. As we choose to love and express it in practical ways, we are creating a climate where sexual intimacy can grow.

Privacy

A fourth principle is: Privacy leads to relaxation. Sexual intercourse is a private act. As we have noted from Scripture, it is the unique expression of love and commitment that a husband and wife have for each other. It is their act of celebration and bonding. To share it with the world is to lose it. The impulse to share either the joys or the struggles of your sexual relationship with friends outside the marriage will likely diminish the joy and increase the struggles. The best place to share sexual struggles is with a marriage counselor not with friends. Certainly we can talk about sex in a public forum. We can explain the male and female anatomy and the role various anatomical organs play in sexual intercourse. We can speak openly of these matters, and we should. However, this is quite different from sharing specifics about what you and your spouse do with each other in sexual lovemaking. Graphically describing your private experience to family, friends, or strangers serves no good purpose. Sharing such private information has often been the setting in which lustful thoughts and desires have been born, sometimes leading to affairs.

Assuming couples agree that their sexual experience is to be their own private joy, they may be faced with practical problems. With small houses and curious children, some couples struggle to find privacy. In fact, a lack of privacy has led some couples to a greatly diminished sexual relationship. Though children get blamed for the parents' withdrawal from the marital bed, it is the couple's responsibility to find a way to have privacy so they can share life sexually.

• • •

In summary, mutual sexual fulfillment is the result of a husband and wife each seeking to bring pleasure to the other. When a married couple gives their bodies to each other as the apostle Paul commanded in 1 Corinthians 7:4, they both find sexual fulfillment. When a couple is committed to pleasing each other, they experience the truth of Jesus' words: "Give, and it will be given to you; a good measure, pressed down, shaken together, and running over will be poured into your lap. For with the measure that you use, it will be measured back to you" (Luke 6:38).

Sometimes our difficulty in seeking to please our spouse is rooted in the fact that we have been hurt, wronged, or abused by him or her. If this is the case, then certainly we need to follow the biblical admonition of confronting the spouse in love and seeking reconciliation. Then with true forgiveness, we reach out to express love by seeking to please them again. As two persons commit themselves to please each other, sexual intimacy will become a reality.

Now let's move on to chapter 22 and discuss the fourth crucial area of intimacy for Christian couples—spiritual intimacy.

CHAPTER TWENTY-TWO

SPIRITUAL INTIMACY

In the last few chapters we have been discussing marital intimacy—that sense of closeness that develops between the husband and wife as they share life. We have discussed intellectual, emotional, and sexual intimacy in particular. In this chapter we come to spiritual intimacy. For some couples this may be the least developed area of marital intimacy. For others, this may be a strong area of intimacy. Our purpose in this chapter is to stimulate further spiritual intimacy.

Let me begin by making a distinction between spiritual growth and spiritual intimacy. Spiritual growth is personal. It is that which is transpiring between you and God. Spiritual intimacy, on the other hand, is that sense of closeness that comes when husband and wife share with each other something of their own spiritual growth. The major part of this chapter is devoted to developing spiritual intimacy, but let's begin with a discussion of two important issues: what spiritual growth is, and the necessity of having a spiritual life before we can experience spiritual growth.

Spiritual Growth

What is spiritual growth? The Christian definition is simple. Spiritual growth is becoming more like Christ. Spiritual growth is not to be equated with participation in religious activities. Rather, it has to do with the changing of the inner person: our attitudes, values, and lifestyle.

The idea that spiritual growth is to be equated with "becoming like Christ" is found throughout the New Testament. For example, Paul said, "Make your own attitude that of Christ Jesus, who, existing in the form of God, did not consider equality with God as something to be used for His own advantage. Instead He emptied Himself by assuming the form of a slave, taking on the likeness of men. And when He had come as a man in his external form, He humbled Himself by becoming obedient to the point of death—even death on a cross" (Phil. 2:5–8). The teaching is clear. We are to think as Christ thought and live as he lived.

Paul further emphasized this in 1 Corinthians 11:1 when he said, "Be imitators of me, as I also am of Christ." Earlier in the same letter, Paul said "Therefore I urge you, be imitators of me. This is why I have sent to you Timothy, who is my beloved and faithful child in the Lord. He will remind you about my ways in Christ Jesus, just as I teach everywhere in every church" (1 Cor. 4:16–17).

Paul exhibits spiritual growth. He is saying, "I am following Christ; therefore, you can follow my example. I am teaching what Christ taught; therefore, you can accept it as trustworthy." Some may think that such a statement is highly egotistical. In reality, every Christian should be able to make such a statement, or at least that should be our goal. If we continue to grow spiritually, following the attitudes and behavior of Christ, we should be able to invite others to follow our example as we follow him. It is a high and lofty goal, but it is clearly the goal God has in mind for us.

One of the most common mistakes in the Christian community is to equate religious activities (attending church, reading the Bible, prayer, etc.) with spiritual growth. We assume that if we are involved in the right activities, we are good Christians. We have confused the means with the end. If these activities help us to become more like Christ, then they become the means of spiritual growth.

All of these activities work together to pave the way for spiritual growth. In attending worship services and Bible study we hear the truth about Christ, find the encouragement of fellow believers, and encounter opportunities to serve others. In personal Scripture reading we discover the truth about God, learn from the teachings of Christ, and examine Christ's life closely in the Gospels. It is in prayer that we express our inadequacies and acknowledge our dependence upon God for power to live Christlike lives.

If we closely examine the life of Christ, we discover the qualities and characteristics God desires to build in our lives. Jesus clearly taught his disciples that they were to follow his example. This is illustrated in Matthew 20:27–28 where Jesus said, "Whoever wants to be first among you must be your slave; just as the Son of Man did not come to be served, but to serve." Jesus further emphasized the characteristic of servanthood when after washing the disciples feet, he said to them, "I have given you an example that you also should do just as I have done for you" (John 13:15). After teaching this profound lesson by his behavior, Jesus added, "If you know these things, you are blessed [happy] if you do them" (John 13:17). It seems clear that spiritual growth is not simply gaining biblical knowledge, even knowledge of Christ's teachings. Spiritual growth involves *applying these teachings to life.* Our greatest happiness will be found in spiritual growth—becoming more like Christ.

This brings us to the second issue: spiritual growth presupposes that we have spiritual life. We cannot grow in Christlikeness until Christ's Spirit lives within us. He gives us spiritual life and thus the potential for spiritual growth. It is possible to "get the cart before the horse." It is my opinion that there are many who are trying hard to live good Christian lives, but they are not in fact Christians at all. They have not personally received Jesus Christ as Savior and invited the Spirit of Christ to take control of their lives. Such efforts to be Christlike without the Spirit of Christ are futile. Sooner or later, such a person will become frustrated with his/her efforts and will fall by the wayside.

I have often heard people say, "I tried being a Christian one time, but it didn't work for me." Their assessment is accurate; it is impossible to live the Christian life without the Spirit of Christ. There must be birth before there can be life and growth.

Recently, I was riding in a cab from O'Hare Airport in Chicago to the Sheraton Hotel. I struck up a conversation with the driver, and in due time he said to me, "I went to church for years. I learned the catechism. I thought I was a Christian, but it was only recently that I learned how to have a personal relationship with Jesus Christ. I realized that I had never invited him into my life. Now things are altogether different. I am studying the Bible and growing as a true Christian." This cabbie was illustrating a vital truth: spiritual growth requires spiritual life. Jesus clearly claimed to be God's Son, the Savior of humankind, the Giver of life. If we have confessed our sins and have received Christ as our Savior, we have become God's children (see John 1:12). We now have spiritual life because the Spirit of Christ lives within us, and we have the potential to grow in Christlikeness.

Understanding and knowing God begins at salvation, but it is to continue throughout life. Paul recognized this when he said, "Not that I have already reached [the goal] or am already fully mature, but I make every effort to take hold of it because I also have been taken hold of by Christ Jesus" (Phil. 3:12). Peter instructs us to "grow in the grace and knowledge of our Lord and Savior Jesus Christ" (2 Pet. 3:18).

Spiritual growth is much like marital growth. It takes time, open communication, and commitment. Spiritual growth is the result of our cooperating with the Holy Spirit's work within us. In our own efforts we cannot attain to Christlikeness. It is only as we allow God's Spirit freedom to work in our lives that he can produce the qualities of Christ in us. Paul speaks of this process when he says, "Therefore, brothers, by the mercies of God, I urge you to present your bodies as a living sacrifice, holy and pleasing to God; this is your spiritual worship. Do not be conformed to this age, but be transformed by the renewing of your mind, so that you may discern what is the good, pleasing, and perfect will of God" (Rom. 12:1–2).

Spiritual growth is a process whereby our old thought patterns are transformed into new thought patterns. It does not happen overnight. We receive new life the moment we receive Christ as Savior, but the spiritual growth process involves our cooperation with the Holy Spirit and allowing the attitudes of Christ to become our attitudes. Our responsibility is to offer our lives as living sacrifices to Christ, thus allowing him to perfect his plans in us.

This is why Paul challenged the believers in Ephesus to "be filled with the Spirit" (Eph. 5:18). The grammar of that sentence indicates that we are "to go on being filled with the Holy Spirit." It is continual action. The control of the Holy Spirit in our lives day by day moves us along toward Christlikeness. For maximal spiritual growth, our daily prayer should be, "Father, I yield my life to your Spirit today, to work in me the things that will make me more like Christ. Give me a clearer understanding of your ways as I read the Scriptures, and give me power to follow Christ's teachings."

Reading, studying, memorizing, and meditating on the Bible—with this prayerful attitude—will bring you a growing understanding of God and what he wants to do in your life. The same dependence on the power of the Holy Spirit will enable you to change negative thoughts and behavioral patterns and thus become more like Christ. This is not a mechanical process. It is a genuine, growing relationship with God that satisfies the deepest longings of the human heart. Blaise Pascal, the French philosopher, was right. There is a "God-shaped vacuum" in every heart that only God can fill. When you pursue personal spiritual growth, you create a climate for spiritual intimacy in your marriage.

Spiritual Intimacy

Spiritual intimacy does not require that both husband and wife be at the same level of spiritual growth. However, spiritual intimacy does require a willingness to share something of our own spiritual pilgrimage with each other. This is not easy for some people. A husband said to me recently, "I know that I should talk with my wife about spiritual things, but when our relationship is not right in other areas, it feels hypocritical to start talking about God and the Bible." His statement illustrates the truth that the spiritual cannot be separated from the rest of life. If we have not developed some degree of emotional, intellectual, and sexual intimacy, it may be extremely difficult to talk about spiritual things. However, spiritual intimacy may begin by confession of our failures in these areas and turning to God together, asking him to help us build not only spiritual intimacy but total intimacy in our marriage. Genuine spiritual intimacy always faces problems realistically and honestly. If each of you can have personal spiritual renewal, then together with the help of God you can begin to experience spiritual intimacy, which will radically affect intimacy in every other area of life.

Sometimes one partner may feel spiritually inferior and will have a tendency to draw back from spiritual intimacy. They do not know the Bible as well as their spouse, they have not been a Christian nearly as long, they did not grow up in a Christian home, or they are sometimes embarrassed in a Bible study class when they are asked specific questions about the Bible. To talk about spiritual things is to run the risk of being embarrassed. Thus, their emotional coping mechanism is to simply avoid anything related to the spiritual. From a psychological point of view, this is easy to understand. From a spiritual perspective, however, it can stifle growth.

What we must remember is that the ground at the cross of Christ is level. All of us come to Christ on our knees. We do not become Christians out of a sense of spiritual superiority. We come as needy people, seeking a Savior. Our past does not make us more acceptable to him. It is the "broken and humbled heart" that he does not despise (Ps. 51:17). All Christians are born as "spiritual babes." We then have the responsibility to grow. Remember, spiritual growth is not "knowing more about the Bible"; it is "becoming more like Christ." We need not apologize for our present state of growth. We must be responsible for continuing to grow.

Another reason some couples have found it difficult to develop spiritual intimacy is that past efforts have proven painful. As one husband said, "We tried talking about the Bible, and it always ended up in an argument." Typically such arguments are followed by withdrawal and an unwillingness to discuss spiritual matters in the future. Because we are individuals with different mind-sets, we sometimes disagree on interpretation and application of Scripture. This is inevitable because we are human. Spiritual intimacy does not require that we agree on all spiritual thoughts. It does require that we are willing to share our thoughts and receive the thoughts and experiences of others with an accepting attitude.

Acceptance is not to be equated with agreement. Acceptance recognizes that we are all growing and that growth involves change. My interpretation of a particular biblical passage today may change six months down the road as I learn more about biblical truth. Acceptance means that you give me the freedom to be where I am today even though you may disagree with my present interpretation. Ultimately we are not after agreement; we are after spiritual growth— both of us becoming more like Christ. As we draw nearer to Christ, we will draw nearer to each other, and our goal of spiritual intimacy will be accomplished.

Underlying all of these hindrances to spiritual intimacy is the fact that we have a spiritual enemy; Satan opposes both spiritual growth and spiritual intimacy. If he can keep us floundering in this area of life, he will cripple our effectiveness for God in the world. Whatever method is effective with us, Satan will use it as long as it is effective in hindering spiritual intimacy. Once we discover Satan's tactics and, in the power of the Holy Spirit, resist those tactics, we have victory over Satan's efforts.

The good news is that the Holy Spirit within us is greater than the spirit of Satan (see 1 John 4:4). We do not resist Satan in our own power; we are no match for him. We resist him in the power of the Holy Spirit and on the basis of Christ's payment for our sins and victory over death. Some Christians have come to fear Satan. This is not God's intention. We are instructed to "submit to God. But resist the Devil, and he will flee from you" (James 4:7). Note the order carefully.

We are to submit to God and then to resist the devil. As we rely upon God's presence and God's power, Satan cannot defeat our efforts at spiritual growth and intimacy.

All other aspects of our marriage are deepened or diminished by our relationship with God. Thus, spiritual intimacy should be a priority for Christians. As the psalmist reminds us, "Unless the LORD builds a house, its builders labor over it in vain" (Ps. 127:1).

Methods of Developing Spiritual intimacy

How can we have a growing sense of spiritual intimacy? How can we enhance our team spirit by becoming spiritual cheerleaders for each other, encouraging each other to spiritual growth? How can we live and work as a spiritual team with and for God? Here are five practical avenues that, if worked into the fabric of a marriage, will develop spiritual intimacy.

Conversation

Spiritual intimacy is strengthened when a couple talks and listens during discussions about spiritual matters. The word is *talk* not *preach*. Preaching to your spouse does not enhance spiritual intimacy. It will almost always close the door. In preaching, you are proclaiming "thus saith the Lord." "Listen to me and I will tell you what God wants you to do" are the words of the preacher. Most of us do not respond positively when our spouse becomes our preacher.

The emphasis on talking is on sharing with each other what God is doing in our lives, how we are understanding his voice to us through Scripture and the Holy Spirit, and the changes in our attitudes and behavior because we have heard his Word. Talking is a means of letting the other into our heart, into our inner thoughts about God, and into our relationship with God. Most of us are willing to receive such information when it is not accompanied by a sermon.

Here are some practical ideas to get your conversations started.

1. Once a week, share with each other one thing you have read in the Bible, why it impressed you, and how you are trying to apply the verse to your life.

2. After attending a worship service, share with each other one thing you found helpful or encouraging from the sermon. (Don't waste your time discussing the things you did not like.)

3. Select a book on Christian living. Read one chapter a week and share with each other one thing you found helpful in the chapter that you are trying to apply to your life.

4. Share one question you have about an aspect of the Bible or Christian living. Attentively listen as your spouse shares any insights about your question.

Remember that listening is fully as important as talking. When your spouse shares something with you, listen attentively, focusing on her with eye contact, nodding the head, leaning forward, and so forth. Be accepting and not condemning of what she is sharing. Accept what she shares as simply her ideas at the moment. If you have a different interpretation of the passage and feel compelled to share it, share it as your interpretation, not as the latest word from God or "Dr. So and So." That is the fastest way to stop communication about spiritual ideas. When you share spiritual insights, talk about how these insights are helping you in your life, not how you wish your spouse would apply this idea to his life. Leave room for the Holy Spirit to work in the heart of your mate. Do not try to do God's work yourself.

One wife said, "I would talk about spiritual things if I thought my husband was interested, but I am not going to compete with the TV." Her statement draws attention to the need for a covenant agreement between husband and wife to discuss spiritual issues. A couple cannot build spiritual intimacy unless both spouses are willing to commit to walk the road together. When I make such a commitment, I am being encouraged to give full attention when my wife chooses to share with me some experience of spiritual growth. I am interested in what she wishes to share because I want to be close to her. I want to enter into her spiritual growth. I want to encourage her in her victories and support her in her request for help. The quality of my listening will either build up or discourage my wife's willingness to talk.

One husband with a "Dead Sea" personality complained, "I wouldn't mind discussing spiritual things, but the conversations tend to get lengthy and I don't have time to do my other responsibilities." This is a sincere and legitimate concern on the part of some. The comment may be couched in humor, but the concern is very real. One answer to such a problem is to agree on time limits for any given discussion. The "Dead Sea" will be more enthusiastic about giving undivided attention as the spouse talks for ten or fifteen minutes if he/she knows that it will not develop into a two-hour conversation.

Do not feel that you can share only the areas of spiritual life in which you are becoming more Christlike. Also share some of the occasions when you are not so Christlike, and ask your spouse to pray for you. Spiritual intimacy does not demand spiritual perfection. Remember that your objective in sharing is not to solve theological problems or to straighten out each other. Your objective is to encourage each other in the challenges God is placing before each of you to become more Christlike.

Praying Together

For a number of years I have taught a "preparation for marriage" class in our church. As a part of this class, I have taught couples how to pray together conversationally. Conversational prayer involves praying about one subject at a time, each sharing a sentence or two about that particular need, and then moving to the next need. Conversational prayer flows from topic to topic, much like a conversation with a friend. After a brief demonstration of this type of prayer, I put each couple in a separate room and ask them to pray aloud conversationally for five minutes. Then I bring the couples back to the larger group and ask, "How did you feel when you started praying together?" Almost always some will say, "nervous," "uncomfortable," or "scared." I then ask, "How did you feel by the time you had completed the five-minute prayer time?" to which most respond, "close," "comfortable," "reluctant to close the prayer," or "relaxed." Praying together tends to develop a sense of spiritual intimacy.

When we come to God together, we are also drawn closer to one another.

Praying together holds great potential for spiritual intimacy. Perhaps that is why it is so difficult for some couples to do. When we pray together, we consciously come to God and share our thoughts and feelings with him. We offer praise and thanksgiving, and we make requests and petitions.

On the other hand, some individuals have never developed the ability to pray aloud in the presence of another person. In that case, my suggestion is that you pray silently. Hold hands; close your eyes; pray silently. And when you have finished praying, say "Amen" aloud. Wait until your spouse says "Amen" aloud, and you have prayed together. God hears silent prayers as well as audible prayers.

When prayer is offered in a public meeting (church service, banquet, etc.), you can deepen your spiritual intimacy by holding hands during the prayer. Joining hands symbolizes joining hearts as you pray along with the one who is leading in public prayer. Praying together enhances not only our relationship with God but our sense of spiritual intimacy.

The method of prayer is not important. What is important is that we come to God together. There is something about the experience of praying together that unites hearts. We feel closer to each other and closer to God. Few spiritual exercises hold as great potential for spiritual intimacy as praying together.

In your private prayers, you will also want to pray for each other daily. Be specific in your prayers. Pray for some of the concerns your spouse has shared with you. Discover some of the prayers in the Bible, and pray these prayers for your spouse, especially those that beseech God for spiritual wisdom and power (see Eph. 1:15–23; Phil. 1:9–11). The psalms can also aid you in praying for your spouse. Read a verse and pray for your spouse whatever that verse brings to your mind. Read the second verse and do the same. Continue through the psalm.

Jesus said to Peter, "Satan has asked to sift you like wheat. But I have prayed for you, that your faith may not fail" (Luke 22:31–32). Samuel said, "As for me, far be it from me that I should sin against the LORD by failing to pray for you" (1 Sam. 12:23). These and many other biblical examples admonish us as to the value of intercessory prayer for fellow Christians. If prayer is the means of ministering in another's life, why would we overlook this ministry to our spouse? What would happen in our marriages if throughout each day, whenever our spouse comes to mind, we prayed for them? Why not try this in your life and see?

Some time ago, an elderly wife said to me, "Years ago, I started this practice. Whenever I want to make a request of my husband, I first pray, 'Lord, help him to want to do this.' Then I go to him and make my request." I asked her husband how this worked from his point of view, and he said, "Whenever she makes a request, I first pray, 'Lord, help me to want to do this.' I repeat this prayer several times as I move toward doing what she has requested. Usually by the time I get to do it, I want to do it." I'm not suggesting this as a pattern for all couples, but simply an illustration of one couple who believes that God is concerned about the inner workings of their marital relationship. Perhaps if we did more praying for each other, we would have not only greater spiritual intimacy but less unresolved conflict in our marriages.

Studying the Scriptures

The Bible admonishes us to "be diligent to present yourself approved to God, a worker who does not need to be ashamed, correctly teaching the word of truth" (2 Tim. 2:15). Jesus was the master Teacher. His followers were called disciples or learners. We too are his disciples. The Bible is God's textbook. In it, he has revealed his will for our lives. As we study the Scriptures, we discover how God views the world and our role in it. Spiritual intimacy can be greatly enhanced when a married couple is involved in Bible study together or shares with each other the fruit of individual Bible study.

No book is more amazing than the Bible. It is the compilation of sixty-six books written over a period of approximately fifteen hundred years by some forty different human authors. It was written in three languages, yet when you put it together, it tells one story from the beginning of mankind to the end of human history. No work contradicts the other, but it is all complementary. It is the story of God the Creator and man the creature, of God's great love for us and his desire to have fellowship with us, and of his means of redeeming us from our own sinful acts and welcoming us as his children. No book is more worthy of our attention than the Bible. No book offers more hope or help in daily living.

The Bible claims to be the Word of God: "No prophecy ever came by the will of man; instead, moved by the Holy Spirit, men spoke from God" (2 Pet. 1:21). As Peter said on another occasion, "The grass withers, and the flower drops off, but the word of the Lord endures forever" (1 Pet. 1:24–25). If the Bible is indeed God's word to us, then certainly we should be challenged to read it passionately with a desire to hear what he desires to say to us. As husbands and wives share with each other what they are discovering in their personal study and as they participate in group Bible studies, spiritual intimacy is deepened. Here are some practical ideas for Bible study.

1.   Study your weekly Bible lesson separately. Then share with each other one thing that impressed you about the lesson and one question you had about the lesson. Lastly, discuss one thing that you can apply to your life.

2.   Read a daily devotional book together and share impressions and one question.

3.   Study together *Building Relationships: A Discipleship Guide for Married Couples.*[1]

4.   Enroll in a discipleship training course offered by your church. In addition to the group sessions, discuss each lesson with each other.

Serving God Together

Another way to stimulate spiritual intimacy is to serve God together. Jesus said, "The Son of Man did not come to be served, but to serve, and to give His life—a ransom for many" (Matt. 20:28). The apostle Peter said of Jesus, "He went about doing good" (Acts 10:38). The central motif in the life of Jesus was service to others. His ultimate act of service was the cross upon which he gave himself for the sins of mankind. As his followers, we are admonished: "We must not get tired of doing good, for we will reap at the proper time if we do not give up. Therefore, as we have opportunity, we must do good for the good of all, especially for those who belong to the household of faith" (Gal. 6:9–10).

The great challenge of the Christian life is to give our lives in service to others under God's direction. We become God's hands and feet in our generation. Jesus taught us that when we serve others, we are in fact serving him (Matt. 25:40). Paul, the great apostle, said, "For we are not proclaiming ourselves, but Jesus Christ as Lord, and ourselves as your servants because of Jesus" (2 Cor. 4:5).

If service to God is so central in the Christian life, it must have an important role in developing spiritual intimacy within marriage. Most Christian couples are involved in some kind of Christian service. However, much of our service is done separately from each other. A wife may teach Sunday school while the husband sings in the choir. A husband may be active in church visitation while the wife leads a missions group. Nothing is wrong with this. Certainly much of our service must be done separately; however, spiritual intimacy is greatly increased if we can perform some service projects together.

For many years in the church I attend, we have had husband/wife teams in all of our Sunday school departments, from preschool through adults. This is not only educationally sound for the pupils who are involved but also a tremendous way of enhancing spiritual intimacy for married couples. Many couples have found that short-term mission trips abroad serve to deepen their spiritual ties. I remember a young couple who served with me in a church construction project in a small village in Brazil, working fourteen-hour days and sleeping in a room large enough for only a double mattress on the floor. Twenty years have passed since that mission experience, but that couple has never been the same. They came back with a renewed vision for foreign missions, became active in our mission programs for boys and girls, and still reflect with pleasure on what God did in their hearts as they served together.

Many service projects are informal, without anyone inviting you to serve. You simply observe an opportunity and take it. A church member dies, and you spend three hours together cleaning house for the recent widow or widower before the friends arrive. You and your spouse meet a single parent and agree to take her ten-year-old daughter on a fishing outing. A friend is moving, and as a couple, you spend time helping clean the house after the moving van is gone. An elderly person confined to home needs a visit, and the two of you go together and invest an hour in reminiscing and laughing together. You know of a financial need in the church family, and the two of you discuss it and agree to give a certain amount of money to that family as an act of Christian love. A widow needs her gutters cleaned, yard mowed, or house painted, and the two of you agree to make the time and exert the effort to do it together. In such service not only are you growing spiritually as individuals, but you are also growing a spiritual bond between the two of you that will spill over and enrich the rest of life.

Individual acts of service, which are later shared with your husband or wife, also deepen spiritual intimacy. We cannot do all spiritual service together, but we can share with each other the opportunities God has given us to minister. We can rejoice and encourage each other in our individual ministries. The important factor for marriage is that we share our service projects with each other so that we can pray for each other, encourage each other, and share the joys of the fruit of that service.

Dreaming Together

I talked recently with a man who said, "I am thinking of retiring early. My wife and I want to get involved in some mission projects—building churches, helping in relief projects, and that sort of thing. We have a travel trailer, and we could go for two or three weeks at a time and invest our lives in this way." How exciting to see a man dreaming! Too many of us are looking back rather than ahead. We are grieving over some of the poor decisions we have made in the past or some painful things that have come our way rather than dreaming about what God has for us in the future. Spiritual intimacy is intensified by dreaming dreams together and talking about these dreams. Some of our dreams will come true, and some will never materialize. But the fact that you dreamed together and talked about those dreams will increase your spiritual intimacy.

Dreaming about and planning for specific steps of spiritual growth creates expectancy. Here are some ideas for the future that include opportunities for spiritual growth and service to others.

- Attend a national marriage enrichment conference
- Take a discipleship course
- Volunteer for ministry
- Build or repair a church
- Start a mission
- Include a church or charitable institution in your estate planning
- Go on a mission trip
- Lead a couples' support group
- Cook a meal for a person in need
- Do home repairs for a senior adult friend
- Serve on a church committee

Check the ones that appeal to you. Make your own dream list, and share it with your spouse. You are on a pilgrimage that will last until our Lord returns or until death. God has plans for the two of you, and you are responding to the promptings of his Spirit to accomplish those plans.

Dreaming dreams keeps us from getting bogged down with the failures of the past or the mundaneness of the present. It plants seeds of hope and stretches our vision. Dreaming acknowledges that we cannot pour a lifetime of service into one day or one week, but we can plan to use the days ahead wisely. If we dream and plan, we can make the most of the time that God allots us.

We have not all been given the same opportunities. We are not endowed with the same gifts and abilities, but we are responsible for what God has given us. God has not asked us to do what others are called to do, but he does have plans for each of us. He does not require us to be brilliant or highly educated or superbly gifted. What God does ask is that we be faithful with what he has entrusted to us. Paul said, "It is expected of managers that each one be found faithful" (1 Cor. 4:2).

❧ ❧ ❧

Our relationship with God is central in building a lasting, satisfying marriage. We acknowledge that the Christian life does not end with salvation. The emphasis is on spiritual growth—becoming like Christ. Each of us must be responsible for our own spiritual growth. At the same time, it is God's plan that in marriage we are to share spiritual growth and ministry. By talking, praying, studying, serving, and dreaming, we can accomplish God's purposes. We are not perfect. We are sometimes not Christlike, but we believe that "if we walk in the light as He Himself is in the light, we have fellowship with one another, and the blood of Jesus His Son cleanses us from all sin" (1 John 1:7).

CHAPTER TWENTY-THREE

WHY DIDN'T SOMEONE TELL ME?

It was Saturday afternoon in Tucson. My seminar was over. Couples were beginning to disperse from the auditorium where we had been meeting when Andrew walked up to me, tears running down his face, and said, "Why didn't someone tell me all of this years ago? I have learned more about marriage in the last few hours than I have learned in a lifetime. If I had known all of this, my marriage would have been very different."

I learned later in our conversation that Andrew's wife, Lynn, had walked out three weeks earlier, telling him that she "no longer wanted to be married." Andrew attended the seminar frantically seeking to discover where he had failed. "I'm not sure my wife will give me another chance," he said. "I wish I had known all of this from the beginning."

Tragically, there are thousands of Andrews and Lynns in the contemporary Christian community. Some have attended churches for years. Except for an occasional sermon on marriage, they have received little help in building a Christian marriage. They have never been confronted with the biblical concepts of covenant marriage, and they have no tools with which to build wholesome communication and intimacy. In a practical sense, they are no better equipped than their secular peers. Does this explain why the divorce rate inside the church parallels the divorce rate in secular culture?

What is ironic is that Andrew and Lynn live in a generation that has produced more Christian books on marriage and more marriage enrichment materials than previous generations. The problem is not lack of resources but lack of exposure. Andrew later admitted that before attending my marriage seminar, he had never read a book on marriage, never worked through any marriage enrichment materials, never attended a marriage enrichment retreat, never talked to a Christian counselor, and never discussed his marriage with his pastor. "I thought our marriage was fine," he said. "Until she walked out the door, I never knew she was unhappy."

Those of us who are professional and lay leaders in the church may seek to allay our guilt by assuming that Andrew was simply a naïve husband who should have been more sensitive to his wife's needs. I am not diminishing Andrew's responsibility; however, I was not able to place all the blame at Andrew's feet when I realized that he was an active member of a Christian church for twenty years.

Recently, I met with 200 pastors from many denominations. At the end of my presentation on marriage enrichment in the church, I asked, "How many of you have a staff couple or a lay couple who have been assigned the specific responsibility of marriage enrichment in your church?" Five hands out of 200 were raised. That means that in 195 churches out of 200, no one had even been assigned the responsibility for marriage enrichment. Until this reality changes, the number of Andrews and Lynns in our congregations will continue to proliferate.

If the church is going to make a difference in contemporary culture, there is no better place to start than in calling the church to rediscover the biblical mandate of covenant marriage. My academic background is anthropology, the study of cultures. No culture has ever survived the breakdown of marriage and family. Western culture will not be an exception. If the trends of the past twenty years continue, Western civilization will self-destruct. The family is the basic unit of social stability. When the family structure loses its grip on society, the society itself becomes unstable.

I am deeply convinced that the only hope for changing current trends lies with the Christian church. My vision is that every local church in every denomination will have regular, ongoing marriage enrichment events provided for its congregation. Once Christian marriages begin to take seriously the biblical pattern for marriage, it will become exceedingly attractive to the non-Christian world.

A few years ago when Dr. Ross Campbell and I wrote the book *Parenting Your Adult Child*,[1] we discovered that 87 percent of single adults between the ages of twenty and thirty said, "I want to have one marriage that will last for a lifetime." They have seen their parents divorce; they have felt the pain of abandonment. That is not what they desire to replicate. Of course they have no idea as to how they can reach the aspiration of a lifelong marriage relationship. Man by nature is self–centered, and the desire for a lifelong marriage usually focuses on the individual's realization that that is best for him or her. However, such self-centered thinking is not what produces lifelong marriages.

The Christian church has not only the model of covenant marriage but both the clear instruction from God on how to have such a marriage as well as the indwelling power of the Holy Spirit who enables us to love unconditionally and to give our lives in service to another. These are the essential ingredients for a covenant marriage.

If you are a member of a Christian church, pastor, or layperson, I urge you to pray that God will raise up one couple in your church who will have vision and passion for directing marriage enrichment in your church. If your church already has a couple who have accepted the responsibility for marriage enrichment, pray that God will give them wisdom to plan and execute marriage enrichment events that will change the lives of the couples in your church. This is the place to start.

Marriage enrichment events need not be elaborate or expensive. It can be as simple as bringing together two or three couples who commit themselves to read and discuss a book on Christian marriage and afterward encourage each other in implementing its principles.

Any couple who has a growing marriage can lead others to the same. You need not have a perfect marriage in order to be a marriage enrichment leader. We are all in process. The more we learn, the more we can share with others. Starting where you are, you can enrich your own marriage and be God's instrument for helping others.

At my marriage seminars I encourage couples to take two steps guaranteed to give them a growing marriage. *First,* attend a marriage enrichment event once a year. This may be a weekend marriage seminar or conference. It may be an eight-week class in your local church. *Secondly,* share one book on marriage every year. Earlier in this book, we talked about how to share a book: read one chapter per week and share with each other one thing you learned about yourself in the chapter. It is an easy way to stimulate communication and enhance marital growth. If you are a pastor or lay leader, let me encourage you to do these two things to enrich your own marriage and better prepare you to minister to others.

If you are a pastor, let me also encourage you not to attempt doing all of the marriage enrichment in your church. Pray that God will raise up a lay couple who will take that responsibility. Lead the church to put monies in the budget to send this couple to marriage enrichment seminars and conferences where they can sharpen their skills in leading marriage enrichment. Also, include monies in the budget to help defray the cost of counseling. When couples in your fellowship reach a crisis in their marriage relationship, often couples do not get the help that is available because they feel that they cannot afford the cost. The church should remove this barrier. It is an excellent investment of church finances. Every marriage saved affects hundreds of other couples.

Pastors and lay leaders who refuse to accept the current divorce trends as inevitable but seek to initiate practical ways of training Christian couples in the skills necessary to maintain a covenant marriage can make a lasting difference not only in Western culture but around the world. The success of Christian marriages will greatly impact the kingdom of God not only in this generation but for generations to come.[2]

NOTES

Chapter 19

1. Gary D. Chapman, *The Five Love Languages* (Chicago: Northfield Publishing, 1995).

Chapter 21

1. An excellent resource is *The Gift of Sex* by Clifford and Joyce Penner (Dallas: Word Publishing, 1981).

Chapter 22

1. Gary D. Chapman, *Building Relationships: A Discipleship Guide for Married Couples* (Nashville: LifeWay Christian Resources, 1995).

Chapter 23

1. Ross Campbell and Gary D. Chapman, *Parenting Your Adult Child* (Chicago: Northfield Publishing, 1999).

2. If you have found the content of this book helpful, you may want to utilize the workbook format, *Covenant Marriage: Communication and Intimacy, Couple Guide,* by Gary Chapman and Betty Hassler, published by LifeWay Press, Nashville, TN. It is accompanied by a leader's guide that gives the lead couple practical ideas for facilitating group discussion.